David Ortiz • Jerry Sollinger

SHAPING OUR ENERGY FUTURE

T0303316

Shaping Our Future by Reducing Energy Intensity in the U.S. Economy

Volume I: Proceedings of the Conference

Prepared for the

U.S. Department of Energy

RAND
SCIENCE AND TECHNOLOGY POLICY INSTITUTE

The research described in this report was conducted by RAND's Science and Technology Policy Institute, under Contract ENG-9812731.

ISBN: 0-8330-3343-3

RAND is a nonprofit institution that helps improve policy and decisionmaking through research and analysis. RAND® is a registered trademark. RAND's publications do not necessarily reflect the opinions or policies of its research sponsors.

Cover design by Stephen Bloodsworth

© Copyright 2003 RAND

All rights reserved. No part of this book may be reproduced in any form by any electronic or mechanical means (including photocopying, recording, or information storage and retrieval) without permission in writing from RAND.

Published 2003 by RAND
1700 Main Street, P.O. Box 2138, Santa Monica, CA 90407-2138
1200 South Hayes Street, Arlington, VA 22202-5050
201 North Craig Street, Suite 202, Pittsburgh, PA 15213
RAND URL: http://www.rand.org/
To order RAND documents or to obtain additional information, contact
Distribution Services: Telephone: (310) 451-7002; Fax: (310) 451-6915; Email:
order@rand.org

From May 14 to 16, 2002, senior government officials and stakeholders convened in Arlington, Virginia, for a conference entitled "Shaping Our Future by
Reducing Energy Intensity in the U.S. Economy." The goal of the conference
was to bring together U.S. Department of Energy officials, industrial stakeholders, academia, nongovernmental organizations, and various federal, state,
and local government organizations to discuss options and strategies for the
implementation of a national priority for improving energy efficiency, as stated
in Chapter 4, Recommendation 14 of the National Energy Policy:

> The National Energy Policy Development Group (NEPDG) recommends that
> the President direct the Secretary of Energy to establish a national priority for
> improving energy efficiency. The priority would be to improve the energy inten-
> sity of the U.S. economy as measured by the amount of energy required for each
> dollar of economic productivity. This increase in efficiency should be pursued
> through the combined efforts of industry, consumers, and federal, state and
> local governments. (NEPDG, 2001)

This proceedings report documents the presentations and discussions of the
conference.

THE SCIENCE AND TECHNOLOGY POLICY INSTITUTE

Originally created by Congress in 1991 as the Critical Technologies Institute and
renamed in 1998, the Science and Technology Policy Institute is a federally
funded research and development center sponsored by the National Science
Foundation and managed by RAND. The institute's mission is to help improve
public policy by conducting objective, independent research and analysis on
policy issues that involve science and technology. To this end, the institute

- supports the Office of Science and Technology Policy and other Executive
  Branch agencies, offices, and councils

- helps science and technology decisionmakers understand the likely consequences of their decisions and choose among alternative policies

- helps improve understanding in both the public and private sectors of the ways in which science and technology can better serve national objectives.

In carrying out its mission, the institute consults broadly with representatives from private industry, institutions of higher education, and other nonprofit institutions.

Inquiries regarding the Science and Technology Policy Institute may be directed to the addresses below:

Dr. Helga Rippen
Director, RAND Science and Technology Policy Institute
1200 South Hayes Street
Arlington, Virginia 22202-5050
Phone: (703) 413-1100
Web: www.rand.org/scitech/stpi/
Email: stpi@rand.org

CONTENTS

FIGURES

BACKGROUND ON THE E-VISION 2000 CONFERENCE

The Bush administration has established the development of a national energy strategy as a major priority and established the National Energy Policy Development Group (NEPDG) to craft such a strategy, including the recommendations necessary to bring it about. A key recommendation of the NEPDG was Recommendation 4-14 (Chapter 4, Recommendation 14) of the National Energy Policy, which requests that the

> President direct the Secretary of Energy to establish a national priority for improving energy efficiency. The priority would be to improve the energy intensity of the U.S. economy as measured by the amount of energy required for each dollar of economic productivity. This increase in efficiency should be pursued through the combined efforts of industry, consumers, and federal, state and local governments. (NEPDG, 2001)

As one step in the implementation of a national priority for improving energy efficiency, the Department of Energy (DOE) sponsored a conference, called E-Vision 2002, in Arlington, Virginia, on May 14–16, 2002. The purpose of the conference was to bring together influential national energy officials, industry leaders from the major energy-consuming sectors, and members of the academic and nongovernmental organization (NGO) communities to discuss ways to implement Recommendation 4-14. E-Vision 2002 brought together more than 150 energy experts drawn from the federal, state, and local government; industry; and NGOs.

This report summarizes the presentations and discussions of the E-Vision 2002 Conference. As such, the document recounts the views of participants expressed during the conference and does not explore or subject to critical analysis the opinions that were expressed. Further, the costs and benefits of proposed strategies have not been evaluated.

The conference was divided into four parts. In the first set of sessions, partici-pants set the context and sketched historical trends and possible futures in energy intensity. In the second set of sessions, participants reviewed previous public and private sector experience at reducing energy intensity with the goal of identifying useful lessons; and in the third set, they laid out some options for implementing Recommendation 4-14. The conference concluded with partici-pants describing goals, actions necessary to achieve them, and obstacles that must be overcome in the implementation of a national priority for improving energy efficiency.

THE CONTEXT AND TRENDS

The context for the conference was set by presentations of historical energy in-tensity trends and predictions of the future, and a roundtable discussion with renowned experts from government, industry, and academia.

The modern history of energy intensity has been one of different degrees of re-duction since 1970, and it has divided into three fairly distinct periods: sharp reductions from 1970 to 1985, gradual reductions between 1985 and 1993, and moderate reductions from 1993 to the present.

The trends in the four energy-consuming sectors broadly mirror the overall trends in energy intensity, but directions in some are more ambiguous than in others. The U.S. economy in general is less energy intensive than it was during previous decades. The structure of the industrial sector is changing. The build-ings sector generally followed the national trends with sharp reductions in the 1970s and a leveling off thereafter. Defining the transportation sector is some-what difficult, given the ways in which transportation interweaves with many aspects of the economy; however, it too generally reflects the overall trend. Trends in the electricity-generating sector have been level in recent years.

ROLES

The private sector is crucial to any substantial reduction in energy intensity. The extent to which private firms address this issue depends in large part on how they view it. If energy is seen as a fixed cost, it tends to receive less atten-tion. If, however, it is regarded as a variable cost component of a product, the manipulation of which can lead to large savings, it rises in visibility and in terms of the amount of attention it receives from senior management. Governments also play an important role since they stand at the intersection of policy and implementation. Nonprofit organizations play a role as well, and they offered a number of success stories.

OPTIONS FOR REDUCING ENERGY INTENSITY

Industrial Sector

The industrial sector consumes a substantial fraction of the nation's energy and should hold considerable potential for reducing energy intensity. For example, the aluminum smelting process is energy intensive and old—it has not changed substantially in 100 years. A theme that emerged repeatedly throughout the conference was the need for, and value of, systems analysis and integration for energy efficiency and lowest life cycle cost. Some participants pointed out the difficulty of innovation and the time required to adopt new technologies. Industry tends to prefer incremental improvements to current processes rather than radical ones. Adopting new technologies also takes time. Government can play an important role by pursing a long-term research and development program in conjunction with industry. Real manufacturing energy intensity showed steep reductions from 1975 to 1985, slower reductions from 1985 to the late 1990s, and some increased reductions from the late 1990s onward. Future energy intensity trends in this sector are unclear.

Buildings Sector

Participants noted that this sector also offers great potential for reductions in energy intensity. Energy-saving products have not made much headway, nor have firms paid much attention to systems analysis. Lighting offers a good example of the unrealized potential: energy-efficient lighting systems include energy-efficient fixtures and the creative use of natural light. But tapping that potential is difficult. While an energy-efficient home can save the owner considerable money, that quality is not as important to prospective homeowners as are size, location, and age of the house. Contractors thus lack strong incentives to incorporate energy efficiency in new home construction.

Transportation Sector

The focus in this sector tends to fall on the fuel economy of automobiles, but many factors other than fuel economy influence energy intensity in the sector. These include land use, development, demographics, and transportation trends. Automobile technologies such as hybrid vehicles and fuel cells promise better fuel efficiency. Some conference participants argued that fuel economy, while beneficial, would not yield great savings in energy intensity; a change in the way that transportation is used is required. Also, a change is required among both consumers and manufacturers for them to value fuel economy and efficiency above vehicle luxury.

Electricity Generation

Energy intensity reductions in the electricity-generating sector must take place under sharply increasing demand. Electricity demand is projected to increase, which in the short term will drive up demand for fossil fuels. In the midterm, DOE is helping to produce a multifuel-generation plant that has no net CO_2 emissions, and nuclear power remains a viable option. In the long term, hydrogen seems to be the solution, but much uncertainty surrounds its development and adoption. The need to turn a profit forces current electricity-generating companies to opt for low-risk incremental advances. Some participants believed that a variety of renewable energy products and programs also hold great promise.

CONCLUDING OBSERVATIONS

The concluding session of the conference focused on reviewing the discussions from the previous two days to explore how DOE, other federal agencies, state and local governments, and industry should begin to implement a national priority for improving energy efficiency. Assistant Secretary of Energy David Garman felt that the DOE Office of Energy Efficiency's (EERE's) role was to implement programs that foster leadership in energy intensity reductions in multiple venues, invest in technology development and deployment, and encourage choice and structural change in how the United States approaches energy production and consumption. The leadership must come from both the private and the public sectors to facilitate technology development and foster risk taking. The technology effort must be a robust one and not focus exclusively on a small set of favored technologies to the exclusion of others. He observed too that change will only occur if there is choice. Energy use patterns in the United States are deeply entrenched and difficult to change. Although entrenched, the patterns of energy use vary substantially, and users need a range of options.

Participants made five recommendations to EERE:

- Establish goals and objectives for particular sectors that link the goal of reducing energy intensity to broader goals such as the reduction of greenhouse gas emissions.

- Replicate successful programs by facilitating intra-industry, state, and local communications regarding successful energy efficiency programs.

- Expand successful programs and promote new ones, including those that promote public-private partnerships.

- Pick the "low-hanging fruit" by supporting and advertising mature and commercially available technology.

- Develop multiple strategies because states and sectors differ considerably and no single approach is likely to succeed everywhere.

Participants identified five broad options for consideration in implementing a national priority for improving energy efficiency. The uncertainty of energy supply and demand is foremost. Whatever actions are undertaken need to be taken with this in mind. Also uncertain is the ability of the market to reduce energy intensity predictably.

Limited data will continue to impede analysis of energy intensity reductions. Participants argued that current data collection efforts do not adequately measure many attributes of energy use that are critical to understanding the role of energy intensity in the U.S. economy.[1]

First steps that federal, state, and local governments can take toward establishing policies to implement a national priority for improving energy efficiency include improving data collection and developing the requisite analytic tools, such as those that help to link energy efficiency to economic productivity. Also needed is networking among commercial firms and states to share information and promote programs that have been shown to reduce energy intensity. Additional options discussed at the conference include tax incentives, reduction of regulatory barriers, education programs, and development of a credible energy efficiency rating system.

---

[1]DOE will release shortly a set of energy intensity indicators based on comprehensive data and analysis techniques.

ACEEE	American Council for an Energy Efficient Economy
AISI	American Iron and Steel Institute
BLS	Bureau of Labor Statistics
Btu	British thermal unit
CEC	California Energy Commission
CO_2	Carbon dioxide
DOE	Department of Energy
DOT	Department of Transportation
EERE	Department of Energy, Office of Energy Efficiency and Renewable Energy
EIA	Department of Energy, Energy Information Administration
EPA	Environmental Protection Agency
EU	European Union
GDP	Gross domestic product
GE	General Electric
GW	Gigawatts
ISO	International Standards Organization
kW	Kilowatts
kWh	Kilowatt hour

LCC	Life cycle cost
LED	Light emitting diode
MW	Megawatts
NASEO	National Association of State Energy Officials
NEP	National Energy Policy
NEPDG	National Energy Policy Development Group
NGO	Nongovernmental organization
NYSERDA	New York State Energy Research and Development Agency
PTI	Public Technology, Inc.
Quad	One quadrillion British thermal units
R&D	Research and development
TVA	Tennessee Valley Authority
WRI	World Resources Institute

Chapter One

INTRODUCTION

One key energy efficiency action found in the National Energy Policy (NEP) is Recommendation 14 in Chapter 4 (referred to as Recommendation 4-14), which is that the

> President direct the Secretary of Energy to establish a national priority for improving energy efficiency. The priority would be to improve the energy intensity of the U.S. economy as measured by the amount of energy required for each dollar of economic productivity. This increase in efficiency should be pursued through the combined efforts of industry, consumers, and federal, state and local governments. (NEPDG, 2001)

PURPOSE AND ORGANIZATION OF THE E-VISION 2002 CONFERENCE

The E-Vision 2002 Conference was one step in the implementation of Recommendation 4-14 of the Bush administration's NEP. It convened in Arlington, Virginia, on May 14, 2002, and adjourned on May 16, 2002. The goal of the conference was "to bring together U.S. Department of Energy (DOE) officials, industrial stakeholders, academia, non-governmental organizations (NGOs), and government organizations to discuss options and strategies for the implementation of a national priority for improving energy efficiency, as stated in Chapter 4, Recommendation 14 of the National Energy Policy (NEP)."

HOW THE CONFERENCE PROCEEDINGS ARE ORGANIZED

This proceedings report is divided into two volumes. The first volume summarizes the conference sessions, which fell into three approximately equal segments. The first three sessions addressed context and definitions and the trends in the energy-consuming sectors, and Chapter Two summarizes these discussions. The next set of sessions examined previous experience with an eye to identifying useful lessons, and Chapter Three encapsulates these discussions. The last set of sessions explored options and strategies for reducing energy intensity, and Chapter Four summarizes them. The final chapter describes goals, actions necessary to achieve them, and obstacles that must be overcome. The second volume of the proceedings is on the enclosed compact disc, and it contains the presentations as well as the opening and closing remarks of Assistant Secretary for Energy Efficiency and Renewable Energy, David Garman, and Director of the Office of Science and Technology Policy, John Marburger. Those who did not attend the conference and want more detail than is provided in the session summaries may wish to consult the enclosed disc.

A NOTE ON CONTENT

This report summarizes the presentations and discussions of the E-Vision 2002 Conference. As such, the document recounts the views of participants expressed during the conference and does not explore or subject to critical analysis the opinions that were expressed. In many cases, comments have been attributed to specific conference participants. However, statements made without specific attribution also represent the views of conference participants. Further, the costs and benefits of proposed strategies have not been evaluated.

Chapter Two

ENERGY INTENSITY AND ENERGY EFFICIENCY

This chapter summarizes the contextual material on energy intensity presented during the first three sessions of E-Vision 2002. It provides a brief history of energy intensity and efficiency since 1970 and offers some definitions. It then describes trends in four energy sectors (industrial, buildings, transportation, and electricity generating) and suggests some possible futures. It also lays out several key national and corporate themes discussed by roundtable participants that help shape the broader context component of the conference.

CONTEXT: MODERN HISTORY OF ENERGY INTENSITY AND ENERGY EFFICIENCY

To provide the context for the discussion of actions to reduce energy intensity in the U.S. economy, E-Vision 2002 began with presentations on the history of energy use and economic activity beginning in the early 1970s. Changes in U.S. economic growth, energy prices, and energy consumption patterns have led to the three distinct periods of energy intensity reductions in the U.S. economy: 1970 to 1985, a period characterized by rapid reductions in energy intensity; 1985 to 1993, a relatively stagnant period; and 1993 to the present, a period characterized by moderate reductions in energy intensity. The gross measure of energy intensity, energy consumption per dollar of gross domestic product (GDP) in constant dollars, is depicted in Figure 2.1.

Geopolitical and domestic events in the early 1970s provided the backdrop for the initial period of rapid decline in energy intensity. The Organization of the Petroleum Exporting Countries (OPEC) oil embargo in 1973 drove up energy prices. A recession lowered economic output. Productivity growth slowed from the brisk postwar pace to 1.2 percent per year. The combination of disrupted energy supplies and a weakening of economic expansion resulted in rapid decreases of energy intensity and significant savings.

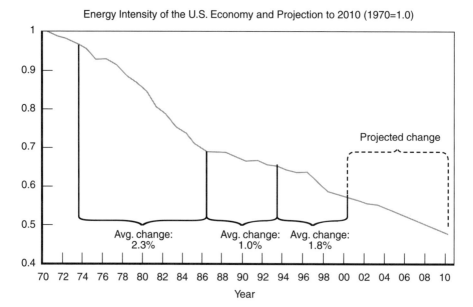

Figure 2.1—Energy Consumption per Dollar of GDP, Indexed to 1970

The economic expansion in the mid-1980s and stabilization of energy supplies and prices eased the pace of reductions in energy intensity. The period from 1985 to 1993 was one of lower energy prices than in the previous decade. Additionally, the composition of the U.S. economy began to shift from manufacturing to services. Consequently, the decline of the gross measure of energy intensity slowed, and the benefits to the economy were marginal at best.

Several factors account for the energy intensity reductions that have occurred since 1993. Since then, the reduction in energy intensity has been approximately 1.8 percent per year, 0.5 percent less than the annual reduction from 1973 to 1985. During the economic expansion of the 1990s, the U.S. economy continued to shift from manufacturing, which had dominated the previous 40 years, to the service industry. Additionally, adjusted prices for energy were lower than they had been in the previous three decades. Lee Schipper of the World Resources Institute (WRI) noted that the combination of structural changes and low energy prices resulted in a relative stagnation of energy intensity in the U.S. economy.

DEFINITIONS AND BACKGROUND

Definitions

Energy Intensity. Ratio of energy consumption to economic or physical output. At the national level, energy intensity is the ratio of total domestic primary energy consumption or final energy consumption to GDP or physical output (EEA, 2002).

Energy Efficiency. The relative thrift or extravagance with which energy inputs are used to provide goods or services (EIA, 1995). It is the ratio of a delivered good or service to the energy consumed in the process.

Background

Tracking progress toward achieving the improvements in energy efficiency requires data. Schipper, and Michael Harper of the Bureau of Labor Statistics (BLS), opened the conference with a discussion of data issues. The various sectors of the economy each use energy and contribute to the economy in different ways, making the collection of data paramount. Analysis of the data must address the characteristics of the energy sectors. Data required to track changes in energy intensity pursuant to implementation of a national priority can be improved.

The DOE Energy Information Administration (EIA) currently collects some detailed data relevant to analyzing energy consumption across sectors of the U.S. economy. However, the EIA surveys occur every three or four years. These surveys include the Residential Energy Consumption Survey, the Manufacturing Energy Consumption Survey, and others. The periodic publishing of the surveys makes time-series analysis, like that used at BLS, difficult to perform with respect to energy consumption. Compounding the problem is the fact that EIA has changed the statistical basis of its analysis several times. The difference in statistical bases makes "apples-to-apples" comparisons of energy consumption difficult.

Changes in data-gathering and analysis techniques recognize the multifaceted nature of energy consumption in the U.S. economy. Site energy, which measures the energy consumed by the end user, is an appropriate measure for some industries, while source energy, which seeks to measure the total amount of energy consumed, including generation, transmission, and delivery losses, is appropriate in other cases. The site/source debate is a longstanding one but highlights the simple fact that the various sectors use energy differently and that the implementation of a national priority for improving energy efficiency needs to take these differences into account.

Similar to the ways in which energy consumption varies greatly across the sectors, so too do the economic contributions. The gross national product (GNP) and GDP are convenient but coarse measures that do not help in policymaking in specific sectors. Fortunately, data regarding economic productivity at the sector level are plentiful due to the efforts of several federal agencies, including BLS.

Tracking economic productivity in the United States has revealed a shift toward less energy-intensive service industries over the past several decades. Sector differences, however, may not reveal differences in actual energy intensity. In a presentation of energy consumption at the state level, Mark Bernstein of RAND attempted to control for shifts in the economic composition of the states to facilitate comparison; the task is difficult. Therefore, while data regarding economic productivity are plentiful, data regarding the energy intensity changes of industries are sparse. Combining appropriate energy and productivity measures into energy intensity measures is critical to the implementation of a national priority for improving energy efficiency.

Both Schipper and Harper noted that energy price has been ignored as a policy tool. Schipper sounded the call early in the conference for transparent pricing of energy in the U.S. economy. During the 1970s—a period of high energy prices—the United States made its greatest gains in energy efficiency and reductions in energy intensity. But these reductions, like those witnessed in California in 2001, might have been short term and due to market conditions and not long-term structural changes. The policy of the U.S. government to guarantee the availability of low-cost energy to U.S. consumers has been so successful that real energy prices are often lower in adjusted dollars than they were a decade ago. The result is that American businesses and consumers have been insulated until recently from elevated energy prices and volatility. European nations and Japan, countries significantly more energy efficient in many measures than the United States, often use energy price as a policy tool. The events of the 1970s suggest that price can be an effective tool for encouraging energy efficiency improvements.

ENERGY-CONSUMING SECTOR TRENDS AND POSSIBLE FUTURES

The second session of E-Vision 2002 called upon U.S. energy officials to present the current state of energy intensity and possible futures in their areas of expertise. Each speaker noted the energy intensity reductions of the 1970s and the stagnation of recent years.

Industrial Sector

Gale Boyd of Argonne National Laboratory presented trends in the industrial sector. The industrial base of the U.S. economy has changed considerably over the past three decades, resulting in net reductions in energy intensity for the sector. The structural shift toward less energy-intense industries has resulted in overall reductions in energy intensity in the industrial sector. The growth of the technology sector has been a primary contributor to the structural change. Boyd noted that reports on success in reducing energy intensity in the industrial sector have been sporadic and anecdotal, perhaps because of the structural changes. Boyd presented a set of possible future energy intensity trends based on EIA's *Annual Energy Outlook*, which he merged with pledges from some private firms. The result was a set of positive projections for large reductions in energy intensity.

Many hurdles must be cleared before the United States has a set of data appropriate for detailed policy analysis of the energy consumption in the industrial sector. Surprisingly, fundamental relationships between energy and the industrial sector are poorly understood. These include the degree to which industries are employing the latest energy-saving technologies and processes, the age of the capital stock, and the relationship of energy to productivity. A goal may be to develop a set of statistics, like those BLS uses, that relates labor to productivity in the U.S. economy. Boyd noted, "In the manufacturing sector, productivity is what is most desired. Energy efficiency is nice and it can help the bottom line, but a better understanding of the linkage between energy efficiency and productivity effects I think would also help us a lot in understanding where we are and where we are going."

Buildings Sector

David Belzer of the Pacific Northwest National Laboratory described trends in the buildings energy sector. The buildings sector is comprised of residential and commercial buildings. Each category contains a number of building classifications, including single and multifamily homes, low-rise and high-rise structures, and others. The sector does not include buildings used for industrial purposes.

Energy intensity in the residential sector mirrored the general trends of the nation. Throughout the 1970s, elevated energy prices contributed to significant reductions in energy intensity in the sector. Changes in heating technology, shell insulation, and behavior all helped. Beginning in the late 1970s and continuing through the 1980s, many states adopted residential energy codes that specified levels of energy efficiency for new and modified structures. Since the mid-1980s, energy price stability has eliminated price as a motivating factor for energy intensity reductions. Little measurable reduction has occurred in energy intensity in the residential sector in recent years, which reveals an apparent paradox: The use of the best current technology for home construction and for appliances could result in a 25-percent reduction in energy intensity. In the 1970s, the differences in technology were not nearly as great as they are now; consequently, energy intensity reductions in the 1970s stemmed from factors other than technology. Using EIA estimates, Belzer showed that the reference case for future energy intensity reductions replicates current trends toward marginal reductions; the use of the best available technology could have a marked effect of a 25-percent or greater reduction. Future reductions in energy intensity in the buildings sector will probably require "significant incentives," according to Belzer.

The commercial sector has exhibited trends similar to those in the residential sector with respect to buildings energy use. Additionally, there has been a marked increase in energy use, primarily for new office equipment. EIA projects few if any gains in the buildings sector with respect to energy intensity using current technology and building techniques.

Transportation Sector

David Greene of Oak Ridge National Laboratory noted that the transportation sector has often been difficult to define precisely, given the way that transportation is woven into various segments of the economy. The transportation sector refers to the moving of people and freight from one location to another. There are many ways of defining energy intensity in this sector, each indicating the productivity of energy in a particular end use. These include energy consumption per ton-mile of freight and energy consumption per passenger mile.

As in other sectors, the elevated energy prices of the 1970s led to a reduction of energy intensity in the transportation sector. The trend continued until approximately 1990, possibly with the help of corporate average fuel economy standards. Since 1990, the energy intensity of the transportation sector has increased. Much of this increase is attributed to changes in passenger vehicles and their patterns of use, which is significant because household transportation use accounts for half of the energy consumed in the sector. Vehicles, on average, are larger and less fuel efficient than they were a little over a decade ago. Also important is the passenger load of vehicles, which is often difficult to analyze. Because the conditions under which previous changes in energy intensity may not be repeated, the historical trends are unlikely to help predict the future. Boyd completed the thought, stating that it is important "to understand the conditions of the past that led to those kinds of changes, and then see whether or not there are issues that make those past changes replicable."

Electricity-Generating Sector

Hillard Huntington of Stanford University presented the electricity-generating sector trends to the conference participants. As mentioned earlier, the distinction between site energy and source energy is critical to the accurate analysis of energy intensity.[1] The distinction is most important in the electricity-generating sector of the economy, where the "product" is a form of energy. This sector consumes 40 percent of the source energy in the United States. The issues surrounding site and source energy affect the transmission, transformation, and distribution of electricity as it travels from the power station to the consumer. Structural shifts in the industry—including industrial consolidation and distributed generation—and market liberalization compound the difficulties in analysis.

The measurement of energy consumption and economic output in the electricity-generating sector must account for a number of factors. These include the generation mix—the portfolio of source fuels that produce electricity serving the region—and the effects of the wholesale power markets. EIA efforts to account for these and other characteristics of the sector include expanding nonutility data and properly disaggregating the different generation types— coal, oil, natural gas, nuclear, hydroelectric, etc. The current measurements indicate that source-specific energy intensity in the sector has not changed in recent years, nor has the overall mixture of source fuels.

To complete the context for E-Vision 2002, industry and university experts engaged in a roundtable discussion to address the broad question, "Where should (or could) we be in 2020 (with respect to reducing energy intensity), and how can we get there?" Henry Lee, director of environment and natural resources at the Kennedy School of Government at Harvard University, introduced several worldviews based on the trend to market liberalization of the energy sector. The first is that the "market will lead us to where we want to be in the year 2020." The second view is that market liberalization may not be able to address the externalities of the environmental cost of energy use and issues of energy security. Markets will be part of the solution, and Schipper noted that "if you believe strongly in the sort of free market view of the world, you have to make sure that the prices are accurate and are providing accurate signals to both producers and consumers." William J. Keese, chairman of the California Energy Commission (CEC) and chairman of the National Association of State Energy Officials, followed Lee's presentation with a discussion of "demand response" on the part of consumers to price signals. Currently, consumers have few

---

[1]Recall that site energy refers to the energy consumed by the end user. Source energy, a broader measure, attempts to capture total energy consumption, including that consumed in generation and lost in transmission.

options with respect to managing their energy costs based on price. It is important that consumers have the control, which will require appliances with controls and timers and real-time metering of energy prices. Roger Platt, senior vice president of the Real Estate Roundtable, presented a broad vision for the future in which the markets that are being formed today are vibrant and healthy, promoting the most efficient energy use possible. To get there, Platt cited the success of the EnergyStar program and programs that underwrite technology risk for builders. Thomas Casten, chairman and CEO of Private Power, LLC, believes that the markets can help us to achieve dramatic reductions in energy intensity, but not the markets that are currently under development. Casten notes that the current markets do not fully liberalize the generation, distribution, and delivery of energy, forming an impenetrable barrier to innovation with respect to energy production and use. Neil Schilke, general director of engineering at General Motors, highlighted the role that advanced technology, clean fuels, and creative partnerships among industry and government are likely to play in achieving improvements in energy efficiency in the transportation sector.

Chapter Three

LESSONS LEARNED FROM PREVIOUS EFFORTS AT REDUCING ENERGY INTENSITY

The second set of conference sessions discussed previous efforts at reducing energy intensity. Participants addressed the factors that caused a particular effort to succeed or fail, so that the lessons could be applied to future efforts. One session was a discussion of private sector experiences at reducing energy intensity. Since the early 1970s, entire businesses have been founded on the premise of energy efficiency. State and local governments often have unique insights into what succeeded in their communities, and a session was devoted to programs at this level. The federal government also played a significant role in setting national policy and often partnered with industrial consortia. Additionally, it had resources that do not typically exist at the state level to implement broad, consumer-based programs. The final session of the "lessons learned" component of the conference addressed these programs.

PRIVATE SECTOR EXPERIENCES

Richard Newell of Resources for the Future introduced the session that discussed private sector experiences at reducing energy intensity. Ultimately, the private sector will play a major role in the implementation of a national priority for improving energy efficiency. The focus of government policy and the partnerships among state and local governments, consortia, and businesses help facilitate the private sector investment in energy-efficient equipment, processes, and products. Many businesses view energy as a fixed cost that is factored into the cost of a product. The transition of energy from an expense to a variable component of a product requires leadership at the executive level. During the session, participants learned that, at Alcoa and Ford, leadership in energy efficiency is helping these firms to save on their energy costs, making them more competitive. Additionally, once energy is a component of a product, energy efficiency itself can be viewed as a service, as it is for Jay Epstein's Health-E-Community Enterprises of Virginia, Inc.

The simplest message regarding energy efficiency for businesses is that it can be profitable. Randy Overbey, president of the energy division at Alcoa, noted that aluminum refining and manufacturing is energy intensive and reductions in energy intensity have been shown to be profitable within one year. This return is significant, given the desire for a positive return on investment by industry. In assembly processes, such as auto manufacturing, plant improvements address energy production and distribution. Improvements include "living roofs" and on-site power and heat generation and distribution. Ford Motor Company has experienced savings of $1.5 million per year at individual manufacturing facilities, according to Susan Cischke, vice president of environmental and safety engineering. Additional benefits of these investments include improved worker comfort and productivity. In any industry, recycling has the potential for dramatic energy savings; recycling metals requires an order of magnitude less energy than production from raw materials.

Intelligent use of energy can be a business. Health-E-Community Enterprises promotes home construction that is based on saving energy and preserving the environment. Epstein has developed a successful business built around the simple concept of meeting a home's energy needs for less than $1 per day. With homes in a number of states, the hallmarks of Epstein's products include natural lighting and air distribution and comfortable, healthier living. These benefits pass directly to the consumer using readily available technology that holds down the cost of construction.

Conference participants noticed a paradox in the panelists' message: If energy efficiency is so profitable, even with today's low energy prices, why is it that so few companies have an avowed commitment to it? The simple answer is inertia: It is always easier to continue along the same path than to make a change. This explanation has several nuances; mentioned above is the fact that energy is considered to be a fixed cost rather than a component of a product. Assistant Secretary Garman noted that the relatively few corporations willing to take the initiative with respect to energy efficiency highlighted a great opportunity to promote information sharing across companies and industries.

STATE AND LOCAL GOVERNMENT EXPERIENCES AT REDUCING ENERGY INTENSITY

State and local governments are at the intersection of policy and implementation. States often form collaborative partnerships with academia and other government organizations and industry. These local and regional partnerships are able to address local and regional problems and issues with local and regional resources. John Nunley, the chair of the session and manager of state energy programs for the Wyoming Business Council, noted efforts in his state at increasing building energy efficiency and those in West Virginia and Iowa for targeting their states' heavy industries in local programs.

Different states have selected different industries for energy intensity reductions because each understands that one size does not fit all. RAND's Mark Bernstein emphasized this point in his statistical analysis of energy consumption and energy intensity. The analysis categorizes states by a number of factors, including industrial mix, weather, prices, and legal and regulatory environment. Table 3.1 lists states in the various groups according to total energy intensity reductions. The three columns, beginning on the left, show states with the largest reductions (greater than 2.2 percent per year), those with the largest reductions in residuals (i.e., the portion of the reduction that could not be accounted for by the various factors considered in the analysis), and those with consistent changes. The goal was to identify states that might offer the most valuable lessons learned about reducing energy intensity.

Brian Henderson of the New York State Energy Research and Development Agency (NYSERDA) described the efforts of his office. The specific experiences of NYSERDA partially explain the challenge of statistical analysis of state-based energy intensity data. In particular, he said, the varied roles of the state energy agency helped to reduce energy intensity on many levels.

Table 3.1

States That Exhibit Special Characteristics in Their Reductions of Energy Intensity

States with the largest energy intensity reductions, greater than 2.2 percent per year	Oregon Washington North Carolina Colorado Delaware
States with largest reductions in residuals, greater than 0.7 percent per year	Oregon Washington North Carolina Kansas Arizona
States that seem to show consistent changes	Washington Oregon Kansas Arizona North Carolina Tennessee

NOTE: The average annual energy intensity change for all states is a reduction of 1.6 percent per year.

The state energy agency wears many hats. It administers funds, regulates, makes policy, and partners with other organizations. NYSERDA administers $201 million of state funds and $617 million in leveraged funds to promote improvements in new building performance. As a regulator, it develops and implements building energy codes and levies fines and penalties when these codes are violated. The Green and Clean building program is an example of the policy role of the state: state buildings must meet stringent energy performance standards, state vehicles are to be 100-percent alternatively fueled, and the electricity generation portfolio is to be 20-percent renewable in the coming decade. New York Executive Order 111 specifies a 35-percent reduction in energy consumption by 2010 and a significant reduction in peak demand. The goals of these policy programs are to jumpstart the market, serve the public good, improve the environment, and stabilize energy prices in a cost-effective manner.

Nonprofit organizations, by their grassroots nature, can also have an effect at the local level. Sharron Brown of Public Technology, Inc. (PTI), and the Urban Consortium Energy Task Force, helps local communities to partner with one another to pool resources, facilitate energy service agreements, and develop effective leadership. Reduction of energy intensity is one goal, but often a subordinate one to reducing a community's energy costs, fostering economic growth, and serving the diversity of local sectors in both the short term and the long term. PTI cites several successful programs as evidence of the power of local programs. The City Lights program in Seattle reduced carbon dioxide output by 68,000 short tons and lowered peak electrical load by 18 MW in 2001. The total savings to consumers of the program were more than $11 million. The program hopes to make similar improvements in 2002. The Cape Light program in Massachusetts formed a regional coalition of municipalities that collectively negotiated better oil, gas, and electricity supply contracts. The result is a great improvement in regional energy reliability. The Business for an Environmentally Sustainable Tomorrow program is similar in its collective approach but addresses a broader set of issues, including water use and transportation congestion in addition to energy. PTI believes that knowledge transfer is the most critical component of success.

FEDERAL EXPERIENCES AT REDUCING ENERGY INTENSITY

Though state and local communities often cooperate with their indigenous industries, the federal government has the most to offer in partnering with industries on a broad scale. Collaboration between DOE and the American Iron and Steel Institute (AISI) provides an example. The steel industry has historically been one of the contributors to the economic growth of the United States and also is one of the most energy-intensive industries. Jim Shultz, vice president of energy and environment for AISI, described the characteristics of his industry. "Steel is energy," Shultz declared: Between 15 and 30 percent of the cost of steel can be directly traced to the energy used to produce it. A steel mill will typically produce its own energy for purposes of reliability and cost. This combination of factors exposes the steel industry to enormous cost risks associated with energy supply. For that reason, AISI is dedicated to raising industry standards across the board, not only for energy but also for waste production, recycling, and safety. Its strategy is codified in a technology roadmap, the implementation of which is cofunded by AISI and DOE. The $23-million program is voluntary and administers more than 25 active projects. Though participation is voluntary, the program has been very successful, and all AISI members will benefit from the results.

Successful partnerships, according to Shultz and John Laitner of the U.S. Environmental Protection Agency (EPA), have a number of characteristics. Because these programs often include cutting-edge technologies, government involvement helps to mitigate the risk to industry and jumpstart a market. Industries must acknowledge the difference between competition and collective action and pool resources for common goals. No program makes sense without a viable business case, and part of that is an explicit statement of realistic goals, verifiable metrics, and implementation timelines. Finally, partnerships need to be flexible to acknowledge the inherent differences among the participants.

The EPA, according to Laitner, views partnerships as a method of improving the energy and environmental performance of American industry in ways other than regulation. Energy efficiency and green power programs are primarily voluntary and include a coordinated set of business and consumer actions. The EPA measures the success of these programs. General economic theory assumes that consumers are making optimal choices, maximizing their return on investment for, say, an appliance. However, this rarely happens in practice, which reveals inefficiencies that the EPA attempts to address with its programs.

A voluntary program, designed and implemented properly, can be very successful. The keys to success are to focus the program on achievable goals and to develop strategic partnerships. These simple techniques have brought the EPA's EnergyStar and Green Power Partnership programs enormous success, Laitner noted. EnergyStar now encompasses more than 30 products and 11,000 individual models. The emphasis on cost-effectiveness has paid off, with a projected return of $70 billion for $13 billion of investment through 2010. The programs have directly addressed consumer decisionmaking but have a collective public benefit. The EnergyStar program has resulted in more than 80 billion kWh saved to date.

Chapter Four

OPTIONS AND STRATEGIES FOR REDUCING ENERGY INTENSITY IN THE U.S. ECONOMY

The final sessions of E-Vision 2002 discussed options and strategies for reducing energy intensity. While government leadership is essential, it is critical to note that the successful implementation of a national priority for improving energy efficiency depends upon the actions of the federal, state, and local governments; industry; and U.S. citizens. The two sessions regarding options and strategies comprised concurrent breakout sessions organized by energy-consuming sector. The first session covered the industrial and buildings sectors and the second session the transportation and electricity generation sectors.

INDUSTRIAL SECTOR

John Green, a consultant, presented options for reducing energy intensity in the aluminum refining industry. This industry is energy intensive, and small gains in efficiency can result in large financial gains. Aluminum production in the United States consumes approximately 1.2 quads of electricity per year. Because of the intensity of the process, smelters often produce much of the electricity that they consume: Thirty-four percent of consumed power is produced on site, and 50 percent of all power consumed by the industry comes from hydropower.

The standard method for producing aluminum in the United States is an old one, and it has considerable potential for decreased energy consumption. The Hall Heroult process is more than 100 years old. Though the theoretical thermodynamic minimum intensity of the process is 6.4 kWh/kg of aluminum produced, the current best practice is approximately 13.0 kWh/kg, and intensity in the U.S. industry ranges from 14 to 18 kWh/kg of aluminum. Incremental improvements to the process include advanced cells that use less energy at higher currents and lower temperatures. Some radical changes to the process include wet and inert cathodes in the production cells.

Several additional steps in the aluminum production process can improve its energy consumption characteristics, Green summarized. Continuous casting of

17

the aluminum product eliminates several rolling steps. More extensive automation with advanced sensors and controls also offers an opportunity for energy savings. Finally, recycling and scrap sorting require far less energy than does refining.

Gunnar Hovstadius of ITT Fluid Technology Corporation focused on what would become a theme of the options and strategies for reducing energy intensity: proper systems analysis and integration of systems for energy efficiency and lowest life cycle cost (LCC). Hovstadius's example was industrial pumping. Since 20 percent of industrial energy consumption can be attributed to pumping, proper design and analysis of the systems are required. However, ITT estimates that 75 percent of pumps are oversized for their application. Since pump efficiencies decline precipitously when pumps are inaccurately sized, the result is wasted energy.

The solution, according to Hovstadius, is to perform systems analysis and consider LCC when designing an industrial system. In the case of industrial pumping systems, that means design the complete system and appropriately size the components. For example, if it is possible to replace a 150-hp motor with a 100-hp motor in a pumping application, the savings over the life of the system can range from $100,000 to $700,000. Smart pumps are available for dynamic applications. This is a low-tech and commonsense solution.

The government may be able to play a role in increasing expertise in industrial systems analysis. The industrial sector consumes approximately one-third of the energy in the United States, and the United States lags behind Japan and Europe in industrial energy intensity, despite gains over the past several decades. Government advocacy and education regarding the value of systems engineering could have a significant effect on energy intensity in the sector. ITT estimates that the adoption of best practices could save $5.8 billion per year in energy costs.

As rapporteur, David Mowery of the Haas School of Business at the University of California challenged the assertions of those describing the industrial sector. His critique raised two points: the uncertainty of innovation and the long process of technology adoption. New technology is often crude and, in the eyes of prospective adopters in industry, compares unfavorably with existing products and long-used processes with which users are quite comfortable. The aluminum smelting process, for example, has existed for a century. The result is that incremental improvements to processes are almost always possible.

Mowery said that technology adoption, similarly, is a process of change. Inefficiencies exist because common users of a technology do not share information. As the ITT presentation showed, isolated pumps are extremely efficient, but there are few applications in which they are applied efficiently. Long-term DOE planning must include a progressive research and development (R&D) portfolio in cooperation with the private sector.

Audience comments focused on the need for DOE leadership. Billy Williams of Dow Chemical, among others, would like to see more international business cooperation. European and Japanese firms have different economic motivations, and there may be many lessons that transfer. Several participants questioned the leadership of American industry. Given the great savings possible with the application of straightforward systems analyses, why does industry fail to embrace it? John Green suggested that a solution to the problem exists in consistent funding of tax credit and incentive programs allowing industry to plan multiyear solutions.

BUILDINGS SECTOR

Though the patterns of energy use in the buildings sector differ from those in the industrial sector, the magnitude of the consumption and the possibilities for gains in efficiency and reductions in intensity are great. In particular, there is little penetration by energy-saving products and little attention paid to appropriate systems analysis. Throughout the discussion, participants stressed that one of the ways in which to improve the productivity of energy use would be to increase communication among architects, builders, owners, and operators.

Fifty-one percent of the energy consumption in commercial buildings and 31 percent in residential buildings is for lighting, began Joseph Oberle of the lighting technology division of General Electric (GE). He presented the efforts of his corporation to advance lighting technology. The performance of lights has improved over the years. Had lighting technology not improved beyond the incandescent lamp, the 7 quads of energy currently used to light America's buildings would be 35 quads. However, even with current lighting technology, energy consumption is expected to increase to 12 quads within the decade. It is possible to counter this trend.

GE continues its development of advanced lighting technology. The standard incandescent light bulb can consume as much as five times the energy as one made with a different technology. Compact florescent bulbs reduce energy consumption by 75 percent when compared with incandescent bulbs and have 12 times the life. Electronically controlled ballasts in commercially available florescent bulbs allow continuous dimming and reduce energy consumption 40 percent compared with standard fluorescents. High-intensity discharge lamps, halogen lamps, and light emitting diode (LED) lamps all promise to save energy consumed for lighting. However, the penetration of these technologies remains low.

Encouraging wider adoption of energy-efficient technologies is difficult. Oberle suggests that multiple programs addressing various consumer groups be adopted. Examples would be the expansion of the EnergyStar program, which has been effective. Homeowner incentives include upgrade and replacement programs. Commercial buildings' energy efficiency can benefit from increased tax incentives for energy improvement. Finally, the government can continue R&D support for advanced lighting technology and control systems to maintain industrial competitiveness and to foster consistent improvements in products.

Mark Ginsberg of DOE made several remarks on barriers to increasing the efficiency of residential housing. Energy efficiency does not add value to the purchase price of a home. This is so despite much evidence that energy efficiency can save a homeowner considerable money over the long term. Size, location, and vintage primarily determine housing value. The turnover in the housing stock is very slow, and many homes cannot be replaced easily with more efficient homes. The contractor base, with the exception of several prominent builders and advocates, does not embrace energy efficiency in new home construction. Finally, system integration—considering the building envelope; lighting; heating, ventilation, and air conditioning; windows; and human behavior when designing the structure—can yield great savings in energy consumption.

Building design begins with the architect, and, if the ideal of a building as an optimized system of components is to be met, then schools of architecture will have to take the lead in training students in these skills. Vivian Loftness, professor of architecture at Carnegie Mellon University, is committed to these goals and articulated them at E-Vision 2002. In her presentation, she noted that a different way of thinking about buildings is required, e.g., the window does not just provide an external view but also lights the room. From her point of view, barriers to better design of buildings include limited research funding at the university level, a desire on the part of builders and building owners to construct at least initial cost, and a misunderstanding of the role that energy services play in improving the productivity of buildings.

Comments from the audience also echoed the theme of system integration. Energy management systems tend to be proprietary, limiting the possibility of a plug-and-play system performing at a high level of efficiency. The bundling of products might persuade consumers to purchase several energy-saving products at once. Promoting technology adoption will be difficult since contractors and owners have little incentive to adopt the creative design of systems. One participant encouraged DOE to use the voluntary nature of the EnergyStar program to push the technological limits of products.

Participants did note that there are many possible solutions to broadening the acceptance of innovative technologies. Encouraging investment in products with paybacks of two to three years would allow many products into the marketplace. Government can play a role by shouldering part of the risk for the adoption of new technologies. Industry and manufacturer partnerships, including manufacturer demonstrations such as the GE Lighting Institute, can also help to encourage market transformation.

TRANSPORTATION SECTOR

Kevin Green of the Department of Transportation's (DOT's) Volpe Center in Cambridge, Massachusetts, introduced the participants to many of the issues facing the transportation sector, focusing on fuel economy. Simple incremental changes in the fuel economy of vehicles are possible in the short term, and DOT partners with many industrial groups to help achieve them. The natural focus in the sector is on automobiles, but civil aviation and freight rail transportation also consume large amounts of energy. However, many nontechnological factors contribute to the energy intensity of the sector. Of principal importance are the relationships among land use, development, demographics, and transportation trends. In the long term, it might be possible to shift the population; in the short term, it is possible to encourage telecommuting. Also important is the fact that transportation use is related to pollution and carbon dioxide (CO_2) emissions, which may eventually be what drives change in the sector.

The automobile and energy industries are among the world's largest industries, and Bernard Robertson of DaimlerChrysler provided an industry viewpoint. Leadership with respect to energy consumption in this sector requires that the government first set definitive goals and timelines to achieve them. Goals may include CO_2 reductions or decreased dependence on foreign oil. Finally, government leadership can help with a sustained commitment to a broad portfolio of short-, mid-, and long-term solutions.

Many automobile technologies that can help to reduce transportation energy intensity are available in the near term. Light-duty diesel engines are popular in the European Union (EU) but difficult to deploy in the United States because of air-quality standards. Most other readily available technologies seek to increase power transmission efficiency: electromechanical automatic transmission and continuously variable transmission systems are two examples.

Mid- and long-term automobile technologies promise greater fuel efficiency but require sustained research and government investment. Hybrid vehicles represent the most readily available midterm technology. Unfortunately, hybrid passenger cars are not cost-effective with current gas prices. Significant deployment may enable equipment prices to decline so that they become competitive, or energy prices may increase dramatically, changing the economic calculus. DaimlerChrysler is developing hybrid vehicles for military use, where the need for stealthy operations and portable electric power make a compelling business case. Fuel cells are the preferred long-term solution but face many obstacles. First, the technology is not likely to be mature until the end of the decade. Additionally, no distribution infrastructure exists for hydrogen, which would be required before large-scale deployment. There may be the option to develop internal combustion, hydrogen-fueled vehicles in the short term, transitioning to fuel cells in the future. Finally, consumer preference requires larger cars with many additional features; many participants questioned Robertson on this point during the session.

Daniel Sperling, founder of the University of California at Davis Institute of Transportation Studies, questioned the assumptions and conclusions of the two speakers. Technological improvements to automobiles—improved internal combustion technologies, hybrid vehicles, and fuel cells—are not going to achieve great reductions in energy intensity. "Technology advances, technology development, [and] R&D are necessary for major improvements in energy intensity and fuel economy, but they are not a sufficient condition," noted Sperling. The problem is also structural. Sperling hoped that information technology could be incorporated into the transportation infrastructure to promote new mobility options, greatly reducing energy intensity. In the words of James Sweeney of Stanford University, the United States has a "transportation monoculture" that is the result of post–World War II U.S. development and continues today. To overcome this problem will require a sustained effort on the part of government, industry, and citizens. The government can focus its efforts on promising but currently unviable technologies that may not be supported by entrenched interests. Industry needs to commit itself to the distribution of advanced technologies, Sperling continued. This begins with putting fuel economy—as opposed to efficiency—above that of greater vehicle luxury. The international auto industry has agreed to a 25-percent increase in fuel economy in the EU but has not agreed to do the same in the United States. The size and influence of the automotive and oil industries give them a bully pulpit that is seldom used: The U.S. automobile industry has a $7-billion advertising budget that "presumably has some effect on the marketplace," noted Sperling.

Participants offered several comments. Fuel prices are critical to market transformation. European countries use taxes and fuel prices to encourage particular behavior in its citizens. Kevin Green raised concerns that price policies may not be applicable in the United States; the technique may not be useful in the United States given the many differences between the United States and Europe. Robertson noted, "Energy is valued in Europe much more highly than it is here." Sperling commented that the natural tendency of consumers is to purchase more in the absence of price controls.

ELECTRICITY GENERATION SECTOR

Roy Hamme, the representative from Duke Energy, pointed out that, like the interstate highway system, the electricity generation, distribution, and transmission system reaches almost every citizen of the nation. Hamme presented an industrial view of options and strategies for reducing energy intensity in the sector. Electricity demand in the United States continues to rise, which in the short term will result in the increased use of fossil fuels. There are short-term technological remedies: advanced, combined cycle, natural gas turbines; fluidized combustion beds; and coal gasification (which costs approximately $1,200 per kW of electricity-generating capacity). In the midterm, DOE is helping to produce the Vision 21 Energy Plant, which will be multifueled and have no net CO_2 emissions during operation. Microturbines are currently inefficient, and fuel cells are extremely costly and unproven in large-scale installations. Nuclear energy remains a viable technology. Superconducting transmission lines could achieve great efficiencies since currently 10 to 40 percent of generated energy is lost during transmission and distribution. As in the transportation sector, the long-term solution appears to be a move to hydrogen; however, its delivery date and ultimate sources remain uncertain. The need to operate profitably forces Duke and others to seek proven, low-risk, incremental advances in technology.

The electricity generation, distribution, and transmission system in the United States can be transformed to help achieve lower energy intensity, Hamme continued. Fundamental changes might include distributed generation, real-time metering, and the differentiating of electricity products, such as different values for peak power versus base load. Industry can and will embrace these changes but only during a period of economic growth and market expansion. Such growth will allow operators to replace inefficient facilities with ones that better react to the new market. Such a change requires a sustained commitment from the government that allows industry experimentation and expansion. One example is the development of combined heat and power plants in the inner city.

Anda Ray addressed E-Vision 2002 on behalf of the Tennessee Valley Authority (TVA). It is mandated to produce the lowest-cost power for its consumers, limiting its ability to invest in some renewable technologies that are quite expensive. Promoting energy efficiency is one component of TVA's strategy for reducing energy intensity. Since 1996, TVA programs have resulted in load reductions of 196 MW. The total costs have been $15 million to $20 million, which results in an effective cost saving per kW of energy of $1,700 to $1,800. It is difficult to make an economic argument for energy efficiency when a peaking combustion turbine costs between $300 and $400 per kW in installed capacity. However, the economic calculus is not as straightforward as it may seem because the benefits of reduced energy costs to consumers are often not considered.

The second component of TVA's strategy is the deployment of cost-effective renewable technology. Currently, TVA has 347 MW of renewable capacity, which seems large until one considers that it represents only 0.2 percent of its total capacity when load factors are considered. The renewable assets include a wind "garden" with 2 MW of capacity and some solar power. The land requirements for biomass generation, approximately 6,000 acres per 10 MW of capacity, preclude its deployment in much of TVA's area. It is possible to expand the percentage of TVA's renewable assets to 5 percent of the total with significant investment.

Significant reductions in energy intensity are possible in combined energy efficiency and renewable programs, Ray noted. Geothermal heat pumps in schools save schools an average of $40,000 per year in energy costs. Hybrid lighting and advanced hot water heaters are available to improve efficiency significantly. Fly ash is being recycled into home insulation. Green pricing of electricity allows different electricity rates to apply to different sources.

There is a distinction between energy efficiency and load management. Energy efficiency in the electricity industry reduces the overall demand and total energy consumption of the sector. It has lasting gains and measurable effects on the energy intensity of the sector, explained Martin Kushler of the American Council for an Energy Efficient Economy (ACEEE). Load management shifts load from peak times, i.e., times during which many of the most expensive generation facilities are in operation, but has only short duration benefits and little effect upon energy intensity.

Because the electricity industry is in the business of selling electricity, it prefers load management to energy efficiency, Kushler noted. Lowering peak demand reduces infrastructure costs but does not reduce overall sales. It allows the power producer to operate its system in an economically efficient manner while consumers continue to use more energy than they need. Current efforts, such as real-time metering and peak load curtailment programs, fall into this category and are unlikely to change energy intensity. A participant noted that it is possible to create a market for energy efficiency.

Government must play a role in the reduction of energy consumption in the electricity-generating sector. "If you're interested in promoting energy efficiency and reducing energy intensity, there is a need for government or regulatory programs and policies to help make that happen," Kushler commented.

Kushler expressed the view that industry has little incentive to lower the consumption of its product. The public benefits of energy efficiency are external to industry and broader than a single consumer, and other private sector entities are not addressing the problem. Industry and government tacitly understand the state of affairs, since the majority of energy efficiency programs were established by legislation rather than by the independent action of industry. Kushler commented that reducing energy intensity is not in the long-term financial interests of the industry. Bill Prindle, also of the ACEEE, picked up on this point with the suggestion that a national public benefits fund based on a fraction of electricity rate charges for energy efficiency might be appropriate.

The rapporteur for the session, Terry Surles of the CEC, tied together the different viewpoints of the speakers with some general thoughts. Market liberalization should not be seen as a panacea: The myriad laws and regulations were developed over the course of a century and cannot be undone with a market or a renewable standard. Many participants agreed that arbitrarily setting a fixed goal for the deployment of renewables would be counterproductive. In fact, markets for varied energy services will not exist until there are standardized connections to the transmission and distribution infrastructure and components interoperate. The U.S. energy supply has many hidden subsidies; the costs of protecting Middle East oil and maintaining the highway infrastructure are two examples. Many improvements are possible from connecting seemingly disparate technologies, including information and communication systems, with the energy system. Finally, there is an enormous potential: In 2001, California reduced its overall electricity load by 8 percent through only behavioral changes, although the situation that sparked the reduction can hardly be regarded as normal.

Chapter Five

ESTABLISHING A NATIONAL PRIORITY FOR IMPROVING ENERGY EFFICIENCY IN THE U.S. ECONOMY

The discussions at E-Vision 2002 brought to light many issues that need to be considered in the implementation of a national priority for improving energy efficiency. Conference topics considered to help clarify those issues included (1) the context for and the historical and possible future of reductions in energy intensity in the U.S. economy, (2) lessons learned at various levels of government and industry, and (3) options for energy intensity reductions in the major energy-consuming sectors of society.

The final session was a working lunch with Assistant Secretary of Energy David Garman. Assistant Secretary Garman led the session, soliciting comments on the appropriate actions for DOE; the DOE Office of Energy Efficiency and Renewable Energy (EERE); industry; universities; and other federal, state, and local government agencies to pursue. The discussion of goals, obstacles, and possible actions provided DOE with many ideas and options to aid successful implementation of a national priority for improving energy efficiency.

ATTRIBUTES OF A NATIONAL PRIORITY FOR IMPROVING ENERGY EFFICIENCY

Assistant Secretary Garman began the session with an illustration of the strategic components of a national priority for improving energy efficiency: Both government and industry must provide consistent leadership; energy efficiency technology must continue to advance; and there must exist an atmosphere that accommodates choice and change in energy services. The Venn diagram in Figure 5.1 illustrates these three components. According to Assistant Secretary Garman, EERE should seek to develop approaches and programs that will result in achieving the intersection: policies and other actions that demonstrate leadership, promote investment in technologies, and encourage choice and structural change. The comments of Assistant Secretary Garman highlighted the

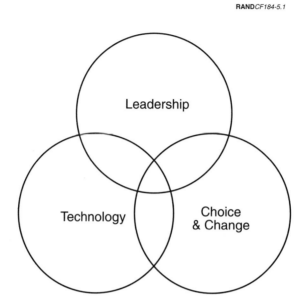

RANDCF184-5.1

Figure 5.1—Attributes of a National Priority for Improving Energy Efficiency

attributes of leadership, technology, and an atmosphere of change and choice because, he observed, they must coexist to promote reductions in energy intensity.

Leadership

"Sustained leadership in both the public and private sectors is critical for success," stated Assistant Secretary Garman. Public and private sector leadership in energy efficiency clears a path that facilitates technological development and promotes risk taking. For example, the EnergyStar program is voluntary and encourages manufacturers to produce and consumers to purchase energy-efficient appliances. This program allows manufacturers to claim a leadership role, promotes the development of technology, and gives information to consumers so that they can make informed decisions. Many previous technology development programs may have been successful in the development of an energy-efficient product but failed to penetrate a market.

Participants at E-Vision 2002 noted that, despite some exceptions, sufficient public and private sector leadership has been lacking. Part of this is the perceived lack of a business case for energy efficiency. But E-Vision 2002 showed that leaders often benefit greatly from these efforts. The support for energy efficiency programs at all levels of government has been inconsistent. When focused, leadership in energy efficiency changes our view of energy use. Several participants warned that leadership can be a double-edged sword—taking a leadership role can be risky and incite criticism. A strategy for implementing a national priority for improving energy efficiency should seek to mitigate this risk.

Technology

The development and deployment of energy-efficient technologies must not put "all of our technology eggs in one basket," noted Assistant Secretary Garman. The technological component of a national priority for reducing energy efficiency in the U.S. economy will deploy currently available technologies and develop the next generation of energy-efficient technologies. Furthermore, the technology portfolio must be diverse. Throughout E-Vision 2002, participants noted that there was a significant amount of "low-hanging fruit," i.e., cost-effective technologies that had not gained market acceptance. Gunnar Hovstadius of ITT described the savings that can be gained through appropriate sizing of pumps in industrial systems. Energy-efficient homebuilders described environmentally friendly home construction techniques and materials that are currently available. Technological development is part of what allows us to achieve greater process efficiencies and is a central component of a priority for reducing energy intensity in the U.S. economy. Throughout E-Vision 2002, the participants noted that revolutionary changes would require a sustained commitment to advanced technological development.

Choice and Change

For new technologies, fuels, and processes to have an effect on the energy intensity of the U.S. economy, businesses and consumers must make a conscious choice to use them. The patterns of U.S. energy consumption are entrenched, and an effort to reduce energy intensity in revolutionary ways will require changes in those patterns. With goals set through effective leadership and technologies developed to achieve those goals, the distribution of those technologies will be the result of choices made over the long term by consumers and industries. Participants noted throughout the conference that "one size does not fit all": The patterns of household energy use differ across the country, the intensity of state economies varies based on climate and industrial mix, the needs of each production facility with respect to reducing energy are unique. The fundamental mechanism through which change will occur is the marketplace for energy services and energy-efficient products. Though there have been notable missteps in the development of markets for energy services, consumer choice is beginning to take root. "The choice genie is out of the bottle," commented

Assistant Secretary Garman. "She is alluring, she is attractive, she is powerful, and she is not going back into the bottle." The existence of choice in energy services allows consumers and business to help mitigate risk stemming from uncertainty arising from energy use. There is uncertainty with respect to the economy; the pace of market restructuring; energy availability; price; security; and the ultimate effects of energy use, including climatic change. To be successful, the market for energy services will require that price accurately reflect the costs of energy consumption. The broader the range of choices that exist, and the easier it is to change energy services, the more successful the national priority will be.

POSSIBLE STRATEGIES OF A NATIONAL PRIORITY FOR IMPROVING ENERGY EFFICIENCY

During the session, there was discussion about what DOE should be trying to accomplish in setting a national priority to improve energy efficiency. The discussion can be summarized by defining five broad areas for DOE programs in the area. Participants felt that DOE should be trying to

- establish goals and objectives

- replicate successful programs undertaken by states and companies

- expand successful programs and start new ones

- pick the "low-hanging fruit"

- develop multiple strategies for multiple sectors.

Goals and Objectives

Throughout the conference, participants noted that energy intensity was a proxy for a number of objectives, and targets for particular sectors and industries should reflect them. One option for implementing a national priority for improving energy efficiency would be for the United States to set targets for energy intensity reduction, either national, sector, or company-level targets. At the conference, participants noted that energy intensity could serve as a proxy for energy efficiency, depending on the level of aggregation at which intensity is defined. Reductions in energy intensity embody broader goals such as greenhouse gas emission reductions, energy security, economic productivity, and environmentally sustainable development. A successful national policy will seek to tie these broader goals to the general goal of reducing energy intensity.

Replicate Successful Programs

A national priority for improving energy efficiency may begin with the replication of successful energy efficiency programs. Representatives of Ford Motor Company and Alcoa described their cost-effective efforts at reducing energy consumption at their manufacturing and smelting facilities. Brian Henderson of NYSERDA described the broad range of programs that his office sponsors throughout New York. Public Technologies, Inc., helps to promote local programs to increase energy efficiency and local and regional energy security. A component of a national priority for improving energy efficiency might include programs that facilitate intra-industry, state, and local communication regarding successful energy efficiency programs.

Expand Successful Programs and Start New Ones

Other programs may be expanded. The EPA/DOE EnergyStar program has been successful in promoting the development, purchase, and installation of energy-efficient appliances, and the range of products that it endorses could be increased. E-Vision 2002 participants also discussed the benefits of public/private partnerships, which included the AISI technology roadmap and lighting technology R&D, for example. These voluntary programs have been low cost to implement and successful at achieving their technology development and deployment goals. New partnerships, based on emerging technologies, may lead to the creation of new successful programs.

Pick the "Low-Hanging Fruit"

The suite of policies and other actions that implement a national priority for improving energy efficiency in the U.S. economy will be a portfolio of programs designed to achieve short- and long-term effects. Participants noted the availability of currently deployable energy-efficient technology and the broad range of "low-hanging fruit" that could be picked. In the transportation and electricity-generating sectors, marginal gains in efficiency can have a large effect. Consumers wield considerable power for increasing energy efficiency in these sectors through behavioral changes. Participants also learned that nearly every energy-consuming application has a proven and cost-effective technology that can help to reduce energy consumption: lighting technology, building materials, and systems-based energy analysis techniques, for example.

Deployment of currently available technology complements long-term, continued development of energy-efficient technologies, and structural changes will help to make continued improvements in the energy intensity of the U.S. economy. Advanced R&D continues in all industries. GE continues to develop high-efficiency lights, the most promising of which are LED technologies. Solar cell development is beginning to yield high-efficiency and cost-effective products. Distributed generation of electricity may help increase efficiency in many areas, but it requires interconnection standards and changes in electricity distribution and pricing. Several participants noted that the patterns of energy use are a direct function of the post–World War II demographic changes in the nation. Materials and methods of building construction require decades to change. A consistent focus on the long-term structural changes is needed.

Pursue Multiple Strategies

There are clear differences in the types of programs and strategies that may be successful in different sectors and subsectors. Recall that "one size does not fit all." The approach to improving energy efficiency in the industrial sector may take a very different path than the approach in the residential sector. DOE should be flexible in its strategies and develop approaches, goals, and strategies for the nation that are appropriate for the different sectors and end uses of energy.

UNCERTAINTIES, RISKS, AND EXTERNAL FACTORS THAT MAY IMPEDE THE ESTABLISHMENT OF A NATIONAL PRIORITY FOR IMPROVING ENERGY EFFICIENCY

The set of policies and other actions that implement a national priority for improving energy efficiency must be developed and placed in a context of numerous uncertainties, risks, and external factors. The participants at E-Vision 2002 highlighted a number of uncertainties and relevant risks that DOE should keep in mind while developing approaches, goals, and strategies to implement a national priority for improving energy efficiency.

Assistant Secretary Garman recalled the warning of an expert, "Daniel Yergin told a group of G-8 ministers in Detroit a couple of weeks ago, 'The only thing you can safely predict about energy in the future is that it will be unpredictable.'" When developing approaches and strategies, DOE needs to acknowledge this uncertainty and incorporate it in policies that can adapt. Also, there is a continuing shift of the U.S. economy toward less-energy-intense, service-based activities that will make it difficult to predict future energy consumption. Energy supplies and demand are uncertain, which will make prediction of prices and volatility especially difficult. Finally, it is difficult to predict the emergence of new technologies, whether they will be adopted and how their adoption will affect energy intensity.

A second uncertainty revolves around the ability of markets to help improve energy intensity. While participants acknowledged that markets would play a significant role in the implementation of a national priority for reducing energy intensity, some expressed doubts regarding how effective markets will be and what the characteristics of future markets will be. Can the market provide incentives for improving energy intensity? Will increased market liberalization lead to increased price volatility, will it meet broader policy goals, and how much government involvement will it require? What role does the government need to play in market acceptance of new technologies?

Problems continue to exist in the collection and dissemination of data regarding energy consumption and its relationship to the economy. E-Vision 2002 participants felt that current energy data systems are not measuring many characteristics of energy use critical to understand the role of energy intensity in the U.S. economy.

Participants felt that the United States can benefit greatly from technologies developed around the world, acknowledging that technological change would not likely occur with U.S. investment only. International cooperation could yield many benefits.

FIRST STEPS IN THE ESTABLISHMENT OF A NATIONAL PRIORITY FOR IMPROVING ENERGY EFFICIENCY

Federal, state, and local governments; industry; and NGOs can take a number of actions to contribute to the realization of a national priority for improving energy efficiency. These include the following:

Collecting Data and Developing Analysis Tools

Throughout E-Vision 2002, participants noted that the appropriate depth of data does not exist to quantify the role of energy at various levels in the U.S. economy. For example, as Lee Schipper noted, the United States is "the only major country that doesn't have a yearly set of national energy accounts for its manufacturing industries." This lack of data translates into a commensurate lack of analysis techniques and sector-specific models that can help in determining the progress of the implementation of a national priority for reducing energy intensity. Consistent collection of appropriate data and the development of metrics and analysis techniques for quantifying the role of energy in the economy—like the data and metrics collected by BLS—is a critical first step.[1]

---

[1]DOE will release shortly a set of energy intensity indicators based upon comprehensive data and analysis techniques.

Networking Among Companies and States

Participants learned of the success of particular companies and states in reducing energy intensity in their activities. An action that may have significant benefits is facilitating communication among businesses, government agencies, states, and citizens. Communication will set the stage for the replication of successful past programs and the development of mutually beneficial partnerships among the public and private sectors.

Additional Options

Assistant Secretary Garman mentioned several additional tools that were discussed at E-Vision 2002. Among the several tools available to help promote the acceptance of currently available technologies are tax incentives for readily available products; regulatory barriers, which can sometimes be reduced to increase the number of options available to businesses; and educational programs, which help to inform consumers about new technologies. Furthermore, the development of a credible and visible energy efficiency rating system, similar to what is currently used in the EnergyStar program and the mile per gallon metric used for cars, can help to create a market value for energy efficiency.

CONCLUSION

Conference attendees concluded that the government must display sustained leadership, support the development of technology, and encourage choice in matters related to energy efficiency. Through adoption of appropriate policies and programs and the promotion of investment, government, industry, and consumers can all help to implement a national priority for improving energy efficiency. Assistant Secretary Garman, in the closing session, summarized these thoughts: "We have to take on this problem in a multidimensional way that focuses on partnerships, that recognizes successes, that encourages leadership, that encourages technological excellence, and that doesn't pursue one thing but many things. That is the challenge that we've got."

CONFERENCE AGENDA

E-VISION 2002: SHAPING OUR FUTURE BY REDUCING ENERGY INTENSITY IN THE U.S. ECONOMY

Sponsored by the U.S. Department of Energy, Office of Energy Efficiency and Renewable Energy

May 14–16, 2002
Crystal Gateway Marriott
Arlington, Virginia

TUESDAY, MAY 14, 2002

12:00 noon	**Registration**
1:00 p.m.	**Opening Plenary**

Chair: *David K. Garman*, Assistant Secretary, Office of Energy Efficiency and Renewable Energy, U.S. Department of Energy

Opening Remarks: *David K. Garman*

Keynote Speaker: *John H. Marburger III*, Director, Office of Science and Technology Policy

Agenda Review: *Douglas R. Brookman*, Public Solutions, Inc.

1:45 p.m.	**SESSION 1: ENERGY INTENSITY CONTEXT**

What are some of the principal factors affecting our ability to reduce energy intensity in the U.S. economy? Presenters will describe energy use vis-à-vis economic productivity and market- and efficiency-based investment decisions. The session will also clarify the challenges of using energy intensity as a proxy for energy efficiency and whether structural factors mask the measure of real efficiency improvements.

Chair: *Abe Haspel*, Office of Energy Efficiency and Renewable Energy, U.S. Department of Energy

Speakers:

"Energy in the Broader Context of the Total Productivity of the Economy," *Michael Harper*, Chief, Division of Productivity Research, Office of Productivity and Technology, U.S. Bureau of Labor Statistics

"What Is Meant by Reducing Energy Intensity, If What We Really Want to Measure Is Energy Efficiency?" *Lee Schipper*, World Resources Institute; Senior Advisor for Transport, Shell Foundation

2:45 p.m.	**Break**
3:05 p.m.	**SESSION 2: HISTORICAL TRENDS AND THE RANGE OF POSSIBLE ENERGY INTENSITY FUTURES**

What are the emerging trends in energy service demands that are important to consider over the next 20 years? What are possible energy intensity futures for the nation and the principal energy-consuming sectors? This session will examine historical and projected changes in energy service demands and energy intensity.

Chair: *Joe Roop*, Senior Research Economist, Pacific Northwest National Laboratory

Speakers:

"Buildings Sector Energy Intensity Trends and Projection," *Dave Belzer*, Staff Scientist, Pacific Northwest National Laboratory

"Transportation Sector Energy Intensity Trends and Projections," *David Greene*, Corporate Fellow, Oak Ridge National Laboratory

"Electricity Generation Sector Energy Intensity Trends and Projections," *Hill Huntington*, Executive Director, Energy Modeling Forum, Stanford University

"Industrial Sector Energy Intensity Trends and Projections," *Gale Boyd*, Economist, Policy and Economic Analysis Group, Argonne National Laboratory

4:00 p.m.   **Open Discussion**

4:30 p.m.	**SESSION 3: ROUNDTABLE DISCUSSION ON REDUCING ENERGY INTENSITY**
	Where should we be in 2020, and how can we get there? Distinguished experts from across the nation representing industry; federal, state, and local governmental agencies; and academia will hold a roundtable discussion on the emerging trends in energy service demand, possible energy intensity futures, and how they might be attained.
	Facilitator: *Douglas R. Brookman*, Public Solutions, Inc.
	Participants:
	William J. Keese, Chairman, California Energy Commission; and Chair of NASEO
	Neal Schilke, General Director of Engineering, General Motors Corporation
	Roger Platt, Senior Vice President and Counsel, Real Estate Roundtable
	Thomas R. Casten, Chairman & CEO, Private Power, LLC
	Henry Lee, Director, Environment and Natural Resources, Kennedy School of Government, Harvard University
6:00 p.m.	**Adjourn**
6:15 p.m.	**Reception**

WEDNESDAY, MAY 15, 2002

8:00 a.m.	**Continental Breakfast**
8:30 a.m.	**SESSION 4: LESSONS LEARNED—PRIVATE SECTOR EXPERIENCES WITH REDUCING ENERGY INTENSITY**
	What works or does not work in the private sector, and why? What do past experiences tell us about the levels of reduction in energy intensity that are possible? The experiences of companies in achieving different levels of reduction in their energy intensity will be highlighted.
	Chair: *Richard Newell*, Fellow, Energy and Natural Resources Division, Resources for the Future

Speakers:

Randy Overbey, President, Energy Division, Primary Metals, Alcoa

Susan Cischke, Vice President, Environmental & Safety Engineering, Ford Motor Company

Jay Epstein, President, Health-E-Community Enterprises of Virginia, Inc.

9:30 a.m.	**Open Discussion**
10:00 a.m.	**Break**

10:30 a.m.   **SESSION 5: LESSONS LEARNED—STATE AND LOCAL GOVERNMENT EXPERIENCES WITH REDUCING ENERGY INTENSITY**

What works or does not work in states and cities, and why? What do past experiences tell us about the levels of reduction in energy intensity that are possible? Presentations will focus on the range of results among some of the state and local governments in reducing their energy intensity. Among the factors discussed will be economic considerations, infrastructure, and climate differences.

Chair: *John F. Nunley, III*, Manager, State Energy Programs, Wyoming Business Council; Vice Chair of NASEO and STEAB Member

Speakers:

Mark Bernstein, Senior Policy Analyst, RAND

Brian Henderson, Program Director, New York State Energy Research & Development Authority (NYSERDA)

Sharron Brown, Public Technology, Inc.; Director, Urban Consortium Energy Task Force

11:30 a.m.	**Open Discussion**
12:00 noon	**SESSION 6: LIGHTNING ROUND**

What are the most compelling features to focus on to establish a national priority for energy efficiency? All conference attendees are invited to participate in brief, small-group discussions of this key question. They should draw upon the information just presented on context, trends and possible future scenarios, and lessons learned from the private and public sectors. After lunch each group will give a brief report back.

Facilitator: *Douglas R. Brookman*, Public Solutions, Inc.

12:20 p.m.	**Luncheon**

2:00 p.m.   **SESSION 6 (continued): LIGHTNING ROUND REPORT BACK**

A representative from each small group will briefly describe one to two leading elements of the group's response to the session's key question. These results will be recorded.

Facilitator: *Douglas R. Brookman*, Public Solutions, Inc.

2:45 p.m.   **SESSION 7: LESSONS LEARNED—FEDERAL GOVERNMENT EXPERIENCES PARTNERING WITH BUSINESS AND GOVERNMENT COMMUNITIES TO FACILITATE ENERGY EFFICIENCY IMPROVEMENTS**

What are the features of federal programs that support private- and public-sector efforts to improve energy efficiency and reduce intensity? To help stimulate discussion, presentations will be made on several federal programs that have been successful in this regard.

Chair: *Steve Nadel*, Executive Director, American Council for an Energy Efficient Economy

Speakers:

Jim Schultz, Vice President of Energy and Environment, American Iron and Steel Institute

John A. "Skip" Laitner, Senior Economist for Technology Policy, Office of Atmospheric Programs, U.S. Environmental Protection Agency

3:45 p.m.   **Break**

4:15 p.m.   **SESSION 8: CONCURRENT BREAKOUT SESSIONS: OPPORTUNITIES FOR TECHNOLOGY AND MARKET CHANGES TO REDUCE ENERGY INTENSITY IN THE INDUSTRIAL AND BUILDINGS SECTORS**

For the industrial and buildings sectors, what are the technologies, research pathways, and market changes that might be needed for future reductions in energy intensity? Speakers will explore this question within each of the concurrent sessions, in light of the specific sector under discussion. The rapporteur for the session will comment on the presentations and offer his/her individual perspective. Ample time will be allotted for open floor discussion.

SESSION 8A: INDUSTRIAL

Chair: *Denise Swink*, Office of Energy Efficiency and Renewable Energy, U.S. Department of Energy

Speakers:

John A. S. Green, Consultant, former Vice President of Technology, The Aluminum Association, Inc.

Gunnar Hovstadius, Director of Technology, ITT Fluid Technology Corporation

Rapporteur: *David C. Mowery*, Professor, Haas School of Business, University of California, Berkeley

5:15 p.m.   **Open Discussion**

SESSION 8B: BUILDINGS

Chair: *Mark Ginsberg*, Office of Energy Efficiency and Renewable Energy, U.S. Department of Energy

Speaker: *Joseph Oberle*, General Manager, Lighting Technology Division, General Electric Company

Rapporteur: *Vivian Loftness*, Professor and Head of the School of Architecture, Carnegie Mellon University

5:15 p.m.   **Open Discussion**

6:00 p.m.   **Adjourn**

6:15 p.m.   **Dinner**

Speaker: *The Honorable Zach Wamp*, Congressman for the 3rd District of Tennessee, U.S. House of Representatives; Co-chairman, House Energy Efficiency and Renewable Energy Caucus

THURSDAY, MAY 16, 2002

7:30 a.m.   **Continental Breakfast**

8:30 a.m.   **SESSION 9: CONCURRENT BREAKOUT SESSIONS: OPPORTUNITIES FOR TECHNOLOGY AND MARKET CHANGES TO REDUCE ENERGY INTENSITY IN THE TRANSPORTATION AND ELECTRICITY GENERATION SECTORS**

For the transportation and electricity generation sectors, what are the technologies, research pathways, and market changes that might be needed for future reductions in energy intensity? Speakers will explore this question within each of the concurrent sessions, in light of the specific sector under discussion. The rapporteur for the session will comment on the presentations and offer his/her individual perspective. Ample time will be allotted for open floor discussion.

SESSION 9A: TRANSPORTATION

Chair: *Edward Wall*, Office of Energy Efficiency and Renewable Energy, U.S. Department of Energy

Speakers:

Kevin Green, Volpe National Transportation Systems Center

Bernard Robertson, Senior Vice President for Engineering Technology, Corporation

Rapporteur: *Daniel Sperling*, Director, Institute of Transportation Studies, University of California at Davis

9:30 a.m.   **Open Discussion**

SESSION 9B: ELECTRIC POWER

Chair: *Robert Dixon*, Office of Energy Efficiency and Renewable Energy, U.S. Department of Energy

Speakers:

Roy E. Hamme, Manager, EHS Issues, Corporate Environment, Health & Safety, Duke Energy Corporation

Anda Ray, Director, Public Power Institute, Tennessee Valley Authority

Marty Kushler, Director, Utility Programs at American Council for an Energy-Efficient Economy

Rapporteur: *Terry Surles*, Director, Technology Systems Division, California Energy Commission

9:30 a.m.   **Open Discussion**

10:15 a.m.   **Break**

10:45 a.m.   **SESSION 10: REPORTS FROM THE CONCURRENT SESSIONS AND OPEN FLOOR DISCUSSION**

Chairs of sessions 8 and 9 will provide five-minute reports conveying the key points from the breakout sessions. The floor will then be open for additional comments from participants, with a focus on the question, *"What could be done to achieve further reductions in energy intensity, and how?"* The chair of this session will briefly summarize this exchange and direct follow-up questions to the appropriate chair of the concurrent sessions, or to members of the audience.

Chair: *James L. Sweeney*, Professor, Management Science and Engineering, and Senior Fellow, Stanford Institute for Economic Policy Research, Stanford University

Speakers:

Industry, *Denise Swink*, Office of Energy Efficiency and Renewable Energy, U.S. Department of Energy

Buildings, *Mark Ginsberg*, Office of Energy Efficiency and Renewable Energy, U.S. Department of Energy

Transportation, *Edward Wall*, Office of Energy Efficiency and Renewable Energy, U.S. Department of Energy

Electricity Generation, *Robert Dixon*, Office of Energy Efficiency and Renewable Energy, U.S. Department of Energy

11:15 a.m.   **Open Discussion**

12:00 noon   **SESSION 11: WORKING LUNCHEON**

SPECIAL TOPIC: IDEAS AND OPTIONS FOR ESTABLISHING A NATIONAL PRIORITY FOR ENERGY EFFICIENCY

This luncheon session will focus on the question, *"How should we begin to establish a national priority for energy efficiency?"* Assistant Secretary David Garman will make a presentation to synthesize the conference proceedings. This will be immediately followed by an open discussion to help Mr. Garman generate the primary outcomes of the conference for presentation to the Secretary of Energy, for his consideration in

establishing a national priority for energy efficiency. In this session, participants will be encouraged to help further define key issues and develop particular ideas, based on their areas of expertise and what they have learned at the conference. This will be a final opportunity to address areas that were not thoroughly discussed or that need more emphasis.

Moderator: *Douglas R. Brookman*, Public Solutions, Inc.

Speaker: "Reflections on Establishing a National Priority for Improving Energy Efficiency," *David K. Garman*, Assistant Secretary, Energy Efficiency and Renewable Energy, U.S. Department of Energy

1:00 p.m.   **Open Discussion**

2:00 p.m.   **Closing Remarks:** *David K. Garman*, Assistant Secretary, Energy Efficiency and Renewable Energy, U.S. Department of Energy

LIST OF ATTENDEES

Jeffrey Anthony
Manager, Research and Innovation
Wisconsin Electric
231 West Michigan Avenue
P321
Milwaukee, WI 53290-0001

Bill Babiuch
Technology Manager
National Renewable Energy
  Laboratory
901 D Street S.W.
Suite 930
Washington, DC 20024

Sam Baldwin
Chief Technology Officer
U.S. Department of Energy
1000 Independence Avenue S.W.
EE-1
Washington, DC 20585

David Bassett
Scientist
U.S. Department of Energy
1000 Independence Avenue S.W.
EE-16
Washington, DC 20585

Stephanie Battles
Survey Statistician
Energy Information Administration
1000 Independence Avenue S.W.
EI-63
Washington, DC 20585

Perry Been
Deputy Director
Texas State Energy Conservation
  Office
111 East 17th Street
Suite 1114
Austin, TX 78701

David Belzer
Staff Scientist
Pacific Northwest National
  Laboratory
2400 Stevens Boulevard
P.O. Box 999
Richland, WA 99352

Charryl Berger
Program Director
Los Alamos National Laboratory
P.O. Box 1663
MS C331
Los Alamos, NM 87544

Jean-Thomas Bernard
Energy Economist and Professor
Energy and Natural Resources
Resources for the Future
1616 P Street N.W.
Washington, DC 20036

Mark Bernstein
Senior Policy Analyst
RAND
P.O. Box 2138
Santa Monica, CA 90407

Darrell Beschen
Chief Economist
EERE
U.S. Department of Energy
1000 Independence Avenue S.W.
EE-3
Washington, DC 20585

Gilbert Bindewald
General Engineer
U.S. Department of Energy
1000 Independence Avenue S.W.
EE-16
Washington, DC 20585-0121

Norman Bliss
Vice President, Technology
American Foundry Society
505 State Street
Des Plaines, IL 60016

Eldon Boes
Director, Energy Analysis Office
National Renewable Energy
 Laboratory
901 D Street
Suite 930
Washington, DC 20024-2157

David Boomsa
U.S. Department of Energy
1000 Independence Avenue S.W.
Washington, DC 20585

Raymond Bougher
M. C. Dean Incorporated
3725 Concorde Parkway
Suite 100
Chantilly, VA 20151

Gale Boyd
Argonne National Laboratory
9700 South Cass Avenue
Argonne, IL 60439

John Boyes
Manager, Energy Infrastructure and
 DER
Sandia National Laboratories
P.O. Box 5800
MS 0710
Albuquerque, NM 87185-0703

Doug Brookman
Facilitator
Public Solutions
23 Bloomsbury Avenue
Baltimore, MD 21228

Michael Brower
Director, Community and
  Governmental Relations
President's Office
SUNY College of Environmental
  Science and Forestry
1 Forestry Drive
Syracuse, NY 13210

Marilyn Brown
Director, Energy Efficiency and
  Renewable Energy Program
Oak Ridge National Laboratory
P.O. Box 2008
1 Bethel Valley Road
Oak Ridge, TN 37831-6186

Sharron Brown
Director of Energy Programs
Public Technology Incorporated
1301 Pennsylvania Avenue N.W.
Washington, DC 20004

Mark Case
President
Etc. Group Incorporated
3481 South 2300 East
Salt Lake City, UT 84109

Thomas Casten
Chairman and CEO
Private Power, LLC
2000 York Road
Suite 129
Oak Brook, IL 60523

Elizabeth Cecchetti
Consultant
Pacific Northwest National
  Laboratory
10420 Greenacres Drive
Silver Spring, MD 20903

Stanley Chen
Engineer
Fossil Energy
U.S. Department of Energy
19901 Germantown Road
Germantown, MD 20874

Susan Cischke
Vice President, Environmental and
  Safety Engineering
Ford Motor Company
1 American Road
12th Floor
Dearborn, MI 48126

Vicki Arroyo Cochran
Director, Policy Analysis
Pew Center on Global Climate
  Change
2101 Wilson Boulevard
Suite 550
Arlington, VA 22201

Brian Connor
Office Director
U.S. Department of Energy
1000 Independence Avenue S.W.
Washington, DC 20585

Tom Cors
Senior Environmental Counsel
Altarum
901 South Highland
Arlington, VA 22204

Dennis Creech
Executive Director
Southface Energy Institute
241 Pine Street
Atlanta, GA 30308

Subodh Das
Director
Center for Aluminum Technology
University of Kentucky
1505 Bull Lea Road
Lexington, KY 40511

Jerry Dion
U.S. Department of Energy
1000 Independence Avenue S.W.
Washington, DC 20585

Robert Dixon
Deputy Assistant Secretary
Office of Power Technologies
U.S. Department of Energy
1000 Independence Avenue S.W.
EE-10
Washington, DC 20585

Michael Doucas
Director, Corporate Development
Engage Networks Incorporated
1320 North Martin Luther King Drive
Milwaukee, WI 53212

Jeffery Dowd
Economist
U.S. Department of Energy
1000 Independence Avenue S.W.
Washington, DC 20585

Carolyn Drake
Director, Washington Office
Southern States Energy Board
P.O. Box 34606
Washington, DC 20043

Jay Epstein
President
Health-E-Community Enterprises
3606 Acorn Drive
Newport News, VA 23607

Jacob Fey
Director
Washington State University Energy
  Program
925 Plum Street
Building #4
Olympia, WA 98504

Douglas Fish
Executive Director
Building Codes Assistance Project
1200 18th Street N.W.
Suite 900
Washington, DC 20036

Eugene Foley
Director
Association of Home Appliance
  Manufacturers
1111 19th Street N.W.
Suite 402
Washington, DC 20036

Katya Fonkych
Doctoral Fellow
RAND
1700 Main Street
Santa Monica, CA 90402

Susan Freedman
Policy Analyst
Northeast Midwest Institute
218 D Street S.W.
Washington, DC 20003

Kenneth Friedman
Senior Advisor
Office of Industrial Technologies
U.S. Department of Energy
1000 Independence Avenue S.W.
Washington, DC 20585

Mark Friedrichs
U.S. Department of Energy
1000 Independence Avenue S.W.
Washington, DC 20585

John Friel
Program Director
RAND
1200 South Hayes Street
Arlington, VA 22202-5050

Buddy Garland
U.S. Department of Energy
1000 Independence Avenue S.W.
Washington, DC 20585

David Garman
Assistant Secretary
Energy Efficiency and Renewable
  Energy
U.S. Department of Energy
1000 Independence Avenue S.W.
EE-1
Washington, DC 20585

Douglas Gatlin
Team Leader
U.S. Environmental Protection
  Agency
1200 Pennsylvania Avenue N.W.
Mail Code 6202J
Washington, DC 20460

Mark Ginsberg
Board of Directors
Energy Efficiency and Renewable
  Energy
U.S. Department of Energy
1000 Independence Avenue S.W.
EE-40
Washington, DC 20585-0121

Robin Graham
Group Leader, Environmental
  Sciences Division
Oak Ridge National Laboratory
P.O. Box 2008
MS 6036
Oak Ridge, TN 37831-6036

Paul Grant
Science Fellow
EPRI
3412 Hillview Avenue
Palo Alto, CA 94304

John Green
Consultant
3712 Tustin Road
Ellicott City, MD 21042

Kevin Green
Engineer
U.S. Department of Transportation
Volpe National Transportation
  Systems Center
55 Broadway
Cambridge, MA 02142

David Greene
Corporate Research Fellow
Oak Ridge National Laboratory
National Transportation Research
  Center
2360 Cherahalq Boulevard
Knoxville, TN 37932

Thomas Gross
Board of Governors
U.S. Department of Energy
1000 Independence Avenue S.W.
EE-30
Washington, DC 20585

Roy Hamme
Manager, EHS Issues
Duke Energy
P.O. Box 1006
Mail Code EC12ZA
Charlotte, NC 28277

John Hanson
Director, Integrated Resource
  Planning
Rates and Regulatory Affairs
Northwest Natural
220 N.W. Second Avenue
Portland, OR 97209

Jeffrey Harris
Staff Scientist
Environmental Energy Technologies
  Division
LBNL
901 D Street S.W.
Suite 950
Washington, DC 20024

Ivy Harrison
Mathematical Statistician
Department of Transportation
Bureau of Transportation Statistics
400 7th Street S.W.
Room 3430
Washington, DC 20590

D. M. Haseltine
Senior Engineering Associate
Eastman Chemical Company
P.O. Box 511
Kingsport, TN 37660-5054

Abraham Haspel
Deputy Assistant Secretary
Energy Efficiency and Renewable
  Energy
U.S. Department of Energy
1000 Independence Avenue S.W.
Room 6A-067
Washington, DC 20585

Brian Henderson
Director
NYSERDA
17 Columbia Circle
Albany, NY 12203

John Herholdt
Manager
Energy Efficiency Program
West Virginia Development Office
State Capitol Complex
Building 6
Room 645
Charleston, WV 25305

James Himonas
President
Novitas Incorporated
370 Amapola Avenue
Unit 212
Torrance, CA 90501

Susan Holte
Management and Program Analyst
Office of Energy Efficiency and
  Renewable Energy
Department of Energy
1000 Independence Avenue S.W.
EE-10
Washington, DC 20585

Jim Houston
Executive Vice President
Industrial Heating Equipment
  Association
1111 North 19th Street
#425
Arlington, VA 22209

Gunnar Hovstadius
Director, Technology
ITT Fluid Technology Corporation
35 Nutmeg Drive
P.O. Box 1004
Trumbull, CT 06611

Hillard Huntington
Executive Director, EMF
Stanford University
406 Terman Center
Stanford, CA 94305-4026

Scott Hutchins
Industrial Programs Manager
U.S. Department of Energy
Northeast Regional Office
JFK Federal Building
#675
Boston, MA 02203

George James
Program Manager
U.S. Department of Energy
1000 Independence Avenue S.W.
EE-41
Washington, DC 20585

Ralph James
Associate Laboratory Director for
  Energy, Environment and National
  Security
Brookhaven National Laboratory
Building 460
40 Brookhaven Avenue
Upton, NY 11973-5000

John Jimison
Executive Director and General
  Counsel
U.S. Combined Heat and Power
  Association
1225 19th Street N.W.
Suite 800
Washington, DC 20036

Russell Jones
Research Manager
American Petroleum Institute
1220 L Street N.W.
Washington, DC 20005

William Keese
Chairman
California Energy Commission
1516 9th Street
MS 32
Sacramento, CA 95814

Aleisha Khan
Program Director
Institute for Market Transformation
8305 Donnybrook Drive
Chevy Chase, MD 20815

Tom Kimbis
Associate
TMS, Inc.

Faith Klareich
Director
Aspen Systems Corporation
2277 Research Boulevard
Rockville, MD 20850

Wilfred Kohl
Professor
Director of IEEP
Johns Hopkins SAIS
1619 Massachusetts Avenue N.W.
Washington, DC 20036

Martin Kushler
Director, Utilities Program
ACEEE
2617 Donna Drive
Williamston, MI 48895

John Laitner
Senior Economist for Technology
  Policy
U.S. Environmental Protection
  Agency
Ariel Rios Building
1200 Pennsylvania Avenue N.W.
Mail Code 6202J
Washington, DC 20460

Michael Lawrence
Associate Laboratory Director
Energy Science and Technology
Pacific Northwest National
  Laboratory
P.O. Box 999
Richland, WA 99352

Tom Leckey
Industry Specialist
Energy Information Administration
U.S. Department of Energy
1000 Independence Avenue S.W.
E1-82
Washington, DC 20585

Henry Lee
Director
Environmental and Natural
  Resources Program
Kennedy School of Government
Harvard University
79 John F. Kennedy Street
Cambridge, MA 02138

Leon Loeb
Doctoral Fellow
RAND
1700 Main Street
Santa Monica, CA 90407

Vivian Loftness
Professor and Head, School of
  Architecture
Department of Architecture
Carnegie Mellon University
5000 Forbes Avenue
Pittsburgh, PA 15213

John Maples
Industry Specialist
Energy Information Administration
U.S. Department of Energy
1000 Independence Avenue S.W.
Washington, DC 20585

John Marburger
Director
Office of Science and Technology
  Policy
1650 Pennsylvania Avenue N.W.
Washington, DC 20502-0001

David Meyer
Principal
Electric Issues LLC
3103 Circle Hill Road
Alexandria, VA 22305

Egils Milbergs
President
National Coalition for Advanced
  Manufacturing
1201 New York Avenue N.W.
Suite 725
Washington, DC 20005

Melissa Miller
Program Development
Los Alamos National Laboratory
P.O. Box 1663
MS C331
Los Alamos, NM 87544

Reginald Modlin
Director
Environmental and Energy Planning
DaimlerChrysler
800 Chrysler Drive
482-00-71
Auburn Hills, MI 48326

John Morrill
Energy Manager
Facilities Maintenance Office Support
  Services
Arlington County Government
1400 North Uhle Street
#403
Arlington, VA 22201

John Morrison
Vice President, Operations
Advanced Energy Corporation
909 Capability Drive
Suite 2100
Raleigh, NC 27606

David Mowery
Professor
Berkeley Haas School of Business
University of California
Mail Code 1900
Berkeley, CA 94720-1980

Christina Mudd
Policy Analyst
Maryland Energy Administration
1623 Forest Drive
Suite 300
Annapolis, MD 21403

Jim Mullen
Director of Technical Services
Lennox International Incorporated
1600 Metrocrest Drive
Carrollton, TX 75011

Steve Nadel
Executive Director
ACEEE
1001 Connecticut Avenue N.W.
Suite 801
Washington, DC 20036

Richard Newell
Fellow
Resources for the Future
1616 P Street N.W.
Washington, DC 20036

Bill Noel
Senior Program Manager
Energy Solutions Group
SAIC
8301 Greensboro Drive
E-4-6
McLean, VA 22102

Douglas Norland
Principal Energy Analyst
Energy Analysis
National Renewable Energy
  Laboratory
901 D Street S.W.
Suite 930
Washington, DC 20024-2157

John Nunley
Manager
State Emergency Programs
Wyoming Business Council
214 West 15th Street
Cheyenne, WY 82002

Joseph Oberle
General Manager
Global Electronics and Ballast
General Electric Lighting
1975 Noble Road
Building 328C
Cleveland, OH 44112

Kirsten Oldenburg
Environmental Program Manager
U.S. Department of Transportation
Bureau of Transportation Statistics
400 7th Street S.W.
K11
Washington, DC 20590

David Ortiz
Engineer
RAND
1200 South Hayes Street
Arlington, VA 22202-5050

Madeline Ostrander
Program Manager
U.S. Conference of Mayors
1620 I Street N.W.
Suite 600
Washington, DC 20006

Randall Overbey
President
Energy Division
Alcoa
900 South Gay Street
1200 Riverview Tower
Knoxville, TN 37902

Rusi Patel
Vice President
Xenergy/Kema Consulting
3 Burlington Woods
Burlington, MA 01803

Phil Patterson
Economist
U.S. Department of Energy
1000 Independence Avenue S.W.
EE-30
Washington, DC 20585

George Phelps
Vice President of Government Affairs
NAIMA
44 Canal Center Plaza
Suite 310
Alexandria, VA 22314

Bill Pitkin
Executive Vice President
National Insulation Association
99 Canal Center Plaza
Suite 222
Alexandria, VA 22314

Roger Platt
Senior Vice President and Counsel
The Real Estate Roundtable
1420 New York Avenue N.W.
Suite 1100
Washington, DC 20005

Peggy Podolak
Industrial Technologies
U.S. Department of Energy
1000 Independence Avenue S.W.
Washington, DC 20585

William Prindle
Deputy Director
ACEEE
1001 Connecticut Avenue N.W.
Suite 900
Washington, DC 20036

Patrick Quinlan
Senior Energy Analyst
National Renewable Energy
  Laboratory
901 D Street S.W.
Suite 930
Washington, DC 20024-2157

Saifur Rahman
Professor
Alexandria Research Institute
Virginia Tech
206 North Washington Street
Suite 400
Alexandria, VA 22314

Anda Ray
Director
Tennessee Valley Authority
1101 Market Street
Chattanooga, TN 37402

Bernard Robertson
Senior Vice President
Engineering and Regulatory Affairs
DaimlerChrysler
800 Chrysler Drive
CIMS 484-10-10
Auburn Hills, MI 48326

Amit Ronen
U.S. Department of Energy
1000 Independence Avenue S.W.
Washington, DC 20585

Joseph Roop
Staff Scientist
Pacific Northwest National
  Laboratory
2400 Stevens Boulevard
P.O. Box 999
MS K6-05
Richland, WA 99352

Steven Rosenstock
Manager
Energy Solutions
Retail Energy Services
Edison Electric Institute
701 Pennsylvania Avenue N.W.
Washington, DC 20004-2696

John Ruether
Senior Engineer
U.S. Department of Energy/NETL
P.O. Box 10940
Pittsburgh, PA 15236

Christopher Russell
Senior Program Manager
Industry Alliance to Save Energy
1200 18th Street N.W.
Washington, DC 20036

Bernard Saffell
Product Line Manager
Energy Science and Technology
Pacific Northwest National
  Laboratory
P.O. Box 999
MS K2-44
902 Battelle Boulevard
Richland, WA 99352

Alan Sanstad
Staff Scientist
Lawrence Berkeley National
  Laboratory
1 Cyclotron Road 90-4000
Berkeley, CA 94720

Diane Schaub
Assistant Engineer
Industrial and Systems Engineering
University of Florida
P.O. Box 116595
303 Weil Hall
Gainesville, FL 32611

Schuyler Schell
Office Director
Office of Planning Budget and
  Outreach
U.S. Department of Energy
1000 Independence Avenue S.W.
Room 6B-052
Washington, DC 20585

Neil Schilke
General Director of Engineering
General Motors
300 Renaissance Center
Detroit, MI 48265-3000

Lee Schipper
Co-Director
Climate and Energy
  Program/EMBARQ
World Resources Institute
10 G Street N.E.
Washington, DC 20002

Mark Schipper
Project Manager
Energy Information Administration
U.S. Department of Energy
1000 Independence Avenue S.W.
EI-652
Washington, DC 2058

James Schultz
Vice President, Environment and
  Energy
American Iron and Steel Institute
1101 17th Street N.W.
Suite 1300
Washington, DC 20036

Robert Shelton
Manager
Planning and Program Development
Engineering Sciences and Technology
  Division
Oak Ridge National Laboratory
P.O. Box 2008
One Bethel Valley Road
Oak Ridge, TN 37831

Christine Silver
Analyst
Sentech Incorporated
4733 Bethesda Avenue
Bethesda, MD 20814

Wendy Soll
Group Leader
Earth and Environmental Sciences
Los Alamos National Laboratory
MS J495
Los Alamos, NM 87545

Jack Solomon
Director of Technology Assessment
Praxair
39 Old Ridgebury Road
Danbury, CT 06810

Sigurd Sorensen
Manager, Industrial and Material
  Technologies
Idaho National Engineering and
  Environmental Laboratory
2525 Fremont Avenue
MS 2210
P.O. Box 1625
Idaho Falls, ID 83415

Victor Sousa
Senior Engineer
Montgomery County
101 Orchard Ridge Drive
Gaithersburg, MD 20878

Chuck Spelay
Chief Policy Analyst
Office of Energy Efficiency
580 Booth Street
18th Floor
Ottawa, Ontario K1A 0E4
Canada

Daniel Sperling
Professor and Director
Institute of Transportation Studies
University of California–Davis
1 Shields Avenue
Davis, CA 95616

Jim Sullivan
U.S. Environmental Protection
  Agency
1200 Pennsylvania Avenue N.W.
Mail Code 6202-J
Washington, DC 20460

Terry Surles
Deputy Director
Technology Systems Division
California Energy Commission
1516 9th Street
MS 51
Sacramento, CA 95814

James Sweeney
Professor
Management Science and
  Engineering Department
Terman Engineering Center 323
Stanford University
Stanford, CA 94305-4026

Richard Sweetser
President
Exergy Partners Corporation
12020 Meadowville Court
Herndon, VA 20170

Denise Swink
Deputy Assistant Secretary
U.S. Department of Energy
1000 Independence Ave. S.W.
EE-20
Washington, DC 20001

Marjorie Tatro
Director
Energy and Transportation Security
  Center
Sandia National Laboratories
P.O. Box 5800
MS 0741
Albuquerque, NM 87185-0741

James Toscas
Executive Vice President
American Concrete Institute
38800 Country Club Drive
Farmington Hills, MI 48331

Paul Trottier
Program Analyst
U.S. Department of Energy
1000 Independence Avenue S.W.
EE-10
Washington, DC 20585

Phillip Tseng
Chief of Integrated Analysis
U.S. Department of Energy
1000 Independence Avenue S.W.
EE 3.1
Washington, DC 20585

Brian Unruh
Industry Specialist
Energy Information Administration
U.S. Department of Energy
1000 Independence Avenue S.W.
Washington, DC 20585

Ed Van Eeckhout
Los Alamos National Laboratory
MS F604
Los Alamos, NM 87544

Steve Wade
Industry Specialist
Energy Information Administration
U.S. Department of Energy
1000 Independence Avenue S.W.
Washington, DC 20585

Edward Wall
Manager
U.S. Department of Energy
1000 Independence Avenue S.W.
Washington, DC 20585

Zach Wamp
Congressman for the 3rd District of
  Tennessee
U.S. House of Representatives
423 Cannon House Office Building
Washington, DC 20515-3271

Wayne Watkins
Associate Vice President/Director
College of Business Administration
University of Akron
259 South Broadway Street
Akron, OH 44325

David Weiss
Executive Director
Industrial Center
400 North Capitol Street N.W.
Suite 450
Washington, DC 20001

Edwin White
Dean of Research
College of Environmental Science and
  Forestry
SUNY
200 Bray Hall
Syracuse, NY 13210

I. L. White
Executive Director
ASERTTI
6834 McLean Province Circle
Falls Church, VA 22043

Gene Whitney
Policy Analyst
National Science and Technology
  Council
Office of Science and Technology
  Policy
1400 20th Street N.W.
Suite 608
Washington, DC 20036

Billy Williams
Director
External Science and Technology
  Programs
Dow Chemical
1776 Eye Street N.W.
Suite 1050
Washington, DC 20006

Warren Wolf
President
Warren W. Wolf Jr. Services
8056 Eliot Drive
Reynoldsburg, OH 43068-1318

Ernst Worrell
Staff Scientist
Environmental Energy Technologies
  Division
Lawrence Berkeley National
  Laboratory
MS 90-4000
1 Cyclotron Road
Berkeley, CA 94720

Adriene Wright
Director
Development and Partner Relations
Electricity Innovation Institute
2000 L Street N.W.
Suite 805
Washington, DC 20036

Robert Wright
Portfolio Manager, Power Systems
Fossil Energy
U.S. Department of Energy
19901 Germantown Road
Germantown, MD 20874-1290

Jay Wrobel
Senior Economist
Energy and Environmental Programs
Gas Technology Institute
1700 South Mount Prospect Road
Des Plaines, IL 60018-1804

Martin Yoklic
Research Planner
School of Planning
University of Arizona
Environmental Research Laboratory
2601 East Airport Drive
Tucson, AZ 85749

Mary Beth Zimmerman
Economist
U.S. Department of Energy
1000 Independence Avenue S.W.
EE-31
Washington, DC 20585

Susan Zinga
Director of Energy Policy
Southface Energy Institute
241 Pine Street
Atlanta, GA 30308

European Environment Agency (EEA), Glossary, available at http://glossary.eea. eu.int/EEAGlossary/, accessed August 2002.

National Energy Policy Development Group (NEPDG), *National Energy Policy: Reliable, Affordable, and Environmentally Sound Energy for America's Future*, Washington, D.C.: U.S. Government Printing Office, May 2001.

U.S. Department of Energy, Energy Information Administration (EIA), *Measuring Energy Efficiency in the United States: A Beginning*, Washington, D.C.: U.S. Government Printing Office, October 1995.

_____, *Annual Energy Outlook 2002*, Washington, D.C.: U.S. Government Printing Office, December 2001.